GARDENING

An A to Z of Flowers, Fruits, Herbs, and Vegetables

The Best Advice, Straight to the Point!

Reader's
digest

The Reader's Digest Association, Inc., New York, NY/Montreal

A READER'S DIGEST BOOK

Copyright © 2016 The Reader's Digest Association, Inc.

The Reader's Digest Quintessential Guide to Gardening contains material
first published in *1001 Hints & Tips for Your Garden.*

Library of Congress Cataloging-in-Publication Data
The Reader's digest quintessential guide to gardening : an A to Z of lawns, flowers, shrubs,
fruits, and vegetables / editors at Reader's digest. -- 1st edition.
     pages cm
 ISBN 978-1-62145-291-1 (alk. paper) -- ISBN 978-1-62145-292-8 (epub)
1. Gardening--Handbooks, manuals, etc. I. Reader's Digest Association, issuing body. II.
Title: Quintessential guide to gardening.
 SB450.96.R43 2016
 635--dc23
                                2015025282

We are committed to both the quality of our products and the service we provide to our
customers. We value your comments, so please feel free to contact us.
        The Reader's Digest Association, Inc.
        Adult Trade Publishing
        44 South Broadway
        White Plains, NY 10601

For more Reader's Digest products and information, visit our website:
        www.rd.com (in the United States)
        www.readersdigest.ca (in Canada)

Printed in China

10 9 8 7 6 5 4 3 2 1

With its A-to-Z format, the *Reader's Digest Quintessential Guide to Gardening* works as a colorful encyclopedia. Just turn to the topic of choice, whether it's tulips or lilies, hoeing or herbs. Covering everything from acid soil to zucchini, the hints and tips you'll find here have been culled from leading horticulturists and accomplished home gardeners all over the country. Many of these nuggets are basic gardening tenets, while others are decidedly unconventional. (As we all know, no two gardeners do things exactly the same way!) Any one of them, however, may prompt you to go outdoors and put your gardening talents to work.

CONTENTS

ACID SOIL

Because acids are produced when organic matter decays, most garden soils are somewhat acidic. They become increasingly sour as humus is worked in and chemicals are leached out.

Determine soil acidity before you plant. Acidity is measured by pH. A pH of 7.0 is neutral; any number below is acid, and any number above is alkaline. Check the pH of your soil with a home testing kit (available in garden-supply stores) or send a soil sample to a lab. Your local Cooperative Extension Service can provide information on testing and sampling. For a quick-and-easy soil test, wet a soil sample and add a pinch of baking soda. If the mix fizzes, the soil may be too acidic for most garden plants and vegetables.

Most garden plants prefer slightly acidic soil with a pH between 6.0 and 6.5. This includes such fruits, vegetables, and flowers as apples and raspberries, beans and peas, and pansies and delphiniums. But other plants like more acid. Azaleas, foxgloves, heather, camellias, gardenias, and blueberries, for example, need a soil with a pH between 4.5 and 6.0

To lower acidity in garden soil, apply 2 ½ to 10 pounds of dolomitic limestone per 100 square feet of soil, depending on soil type: a heavy, clay soil will require more amendment than a sandy one. To raise the pH still higher, till the limestone into the top 6 inches of soil. Ashes from the fireplace or a wood-burning stove can also "sweeten" the soil. Spread 5 to 10 pounds per 100 square feet to raise the pH by one unit.

In regions with high rainfall, soils acidify more quickly as calcium leaches through the soil. Even if pH is at the right level, sprinkle the soil with limestone, which will slowly work its way downward.

AGAVE

According to folklore, the century plant (the common name for *Agave americana*) flowers once every one hundred years. In fact, the plant may bloom its first and only time in ten years, then dies. Agaves grown in pots may take even longer to bloom.

A garden guardian. Plant the imposing agave around the perimeter of your property, underneath windows, or at the edges of other plantings. The needle-sharp leaves will discourage intruders and animals. But keep them away from walkways, where their sharp and spiky leaves can become a danger to friend as well as foe.

For erosion control, especially in arid regions, try planting agaves on banks. They also make excellent windscreens when planted around the borders of a large property. They're often unsuitable for limited spaces, however, since their large size can visually dominate an entire landscape.

Climate too cold? Grow agaves, which will remain hardy down to 40°F, outside in containers in summer. When winter comes, store the plants in the basement and keep them dry.

Keep agaves neat and trim by regularly removing the untidy lower leaves. And remember that agaves die after they flower. Remove the entire plant once blooming is completed and the rosettes have died.

ALKALINE SOIL

Add a few drops of cider vinegar to a soil sample. If it fizzes, the soil is alkaline. For a precise reading, contact your local Cooperative Extension Service to learn how to take a sample and where to send it. Or pick up a home test kit online or at a local garden-supply store.

Reduce alkalinity by adding acidic materials such as peat moss, sulfur, or aluminum sulfate to your soil. To lower the pH by one unit, add 5 pounds of peat moss, ½ to 2 ½ pounds of sulfur, or 5 to 15 pounds of aluminum sulfate per 100 square feet. Use the smaller amounts of additives in sandy soils and progressively larger amounts in heavier soils. Improving drainage may help reduce alkalinity by allowing water to wash

Reader's Digest Quintessential Guide

through and carry away alkaline salts. Put plenty of dead leaves, compost, or other organic matter into the bottom of planting holes. Coffee grounds help reduce alkalinity, too. Dig a good helping into the soil. Blanketing the ground with an organic mulch prevents surface evaporation of water and the buildup of alkaline salts.

In western states, alkaline soils tend to be high in sodium, which makes them tight and sticky. Water the soil to loosen it. After it dries, dig in gypsum—about 2 pounds per 100 square feet of moderately clayey soil.

Make the best of it. Instead of acidifying your soil, consider growing plants that like it alkaline. Desirable flowers in this category include the Madonna lily, purple coneflower, phlox, and candytuft.

ALOE

Warmth and sunlight are keys to growing these African natives, so place aloes in full sun—except those with speckled leaves, which need midday shade. Rich soil, good drainage, and regular summer watering are also important. Most species won't survive temperatures below 40°F, so frost protection is often needed in cooler climes.

Add year-round drama to your garden by planting aloes in large groupings. Many species—including *Aloe ferox* and *Aloe brevifolia*—flower during fall and winter when little else does, and mass plantings tend to emphasize the bright display of gold, coral, and orange flowers. Choose small to medium varieties and install them in rows, with each plant 18 to 24 inches apart. The plantings will expand into attractive large clumps within two to three years.

Leave the earth bare around aloes to highlight their striking sculptural quality. And regularly groom older clumps to keep offshoots from cluttering up the plant's inherent neatness and simplicity.

To grow aloes in pots, provide a moist, porous potting mixture by using 2 parts soil, 2 parts perlite or coarse sand, ¼ part bonemeal, and ½ part dehydrated cow manure. Keep your potted aloe at a minimum of 50° to 55°F.

ALUMINUM FOIL

Protect young trees from mice and rabbits. Wrap trunks loosely in sheets of foil to a height of 18 inches. The glittering, rattling surface keeps the gnawers away.

Use aluminum foil mulch to speed growth and protect against insects. Stretch it between rows of plants and use rocks or bricks along the edge to anchor. The light the foil reflects can increase yields, especially in cloudy regions, and speed the ripening of tomatoes or the blooming of a rosebush by a full two weeks. The foil also keeps thrips and aphids away.

A cheap substitute. If you're using large amounts of foil, save money by painting black plastic mulch with the aluminum-colored paint sold at hardware stores.

Foil scarecrows. Keep birds away by cutting patterns from cardboard—stars, circles, seashells—and wrapping them in foil. Hang from the branches of ripening berry bushes and fruit trees.

Cones for bulbs. Give forced crocus and hyacinth bulbs the darkness they need by placing them on a chilly windowsill and covering with a cone of foil. Remove the foil when crocus shoots reach 2 inches and when hyacinth shoots reach 4 inches.

ANNUALS

Purchasing

Young plants in six- or eight-packs of the same variety are often available at very low prices. The seedlings should be well rooted but need not be in bloom. Once planting season is past, however, beware of starved, dried-up leftovers.

Climbing annuals will quickly disguise a chain-link fence or the screening around garbage cans. Morning glory, scarlet runner beans, black-eyed Susan vine, sweet peas, and hyacinth bean are some of the climbers that do the job nicely.

A few for shady gardens: Impatiens, monkey flower, nasturtium, California bluebell, and wishbone flower are shade-tolerant annuals.

For pots and window boxes, choose bushy or trailing annuals. Petunias, marigolds, verbenas, thunbergia, lobelia, and heliotrope are ideal. But avoid tall plants like sunflowers, which look awkward in small containers.

Planting

The right place. A sunny location with good drainage is more important to most annuals than soil quality.

Use as fillers. Plant annuals in the empty spaces between shrubs, foundation plants, perennials, or rows of vegetables.

Sow half-hardy annuals indoors to give them a head start. To make sure they're evenly spaced, place chicken wire over your seeding tray and put a seed in each hole. This makes it easier to separate the seedlings for transplanting.

Flowers all season. While you wait for perennials to take hold, dress up the garden with annuals. Since they germinate, bloom, and die within a single season, there's no need to dig them up once the later flowers are established.

Color considerations. Massing a single color will create an elegant, unified effect suitable for terraces, planters, and window boxes. Pastels—white, pinks, lavenders, yellows—show up best in early morning and evening light. If you want a multicolored effect, make a sketch and color it in; it will help you keep the colors harmonious.

Maintenance

Good and wet. Plenty of moisture is essential when you set out young plants. First, soak them in a tub of water. Plant only after the root ball is thoroughly wet. As extra insurance, soak the planting hole with a good watering as well.

Annuals don't like manure—even when it's well aged. Too much nitrogen results in plants with too many leaves, too many stems, and too few flowers. The only manure suitable for use on annuals is one that has dried for at least two years.

Pinching young plants delays blooming but helps them become stockier and bushier. Annuals such as clarkia, sweet pea, cosmos, godetia, coleus, snapdragon, nicotiana, red salvia, and petunia benefit from pinching. Use your thumb and forefinger to nip out the growing tip of the main stem just above a leaf or pair of leaves.

Which to deadhead. Use shears or scissors to remove dead flowers from annuals that bloom in flushes, like coreopsis, petunias, California poppies, and marigolds.

Put annuals into pots at the end of summer. Species such as coleus, impatiens, browallia, geranium, floss flower, and wishbone flower will provide attractive blooms in your home for several months.

ANTS

Gardeners usually consider ants to be pests. Ants can loosen the soil around young plants, causing them to die. Some species shelter and protect aphids, whose honeydew they feed on. On the positive side, ants can improve air circulation in heavy soils, and their burrows improve water drainage.

To get rid of a colony, cover the anthill with a large flowerpot whose drainage hole has been plugged with a cork or tightly wadded plastic wrap. Heat a bucket of water to boiling and flood the surrounding soil, reserving a few gallons of the water. Wait a minute or two for most of the ants to find shelter in the overturned pot, then turn it upright and pour in the remaining water. Boric acid mixed with sugar is an effective ant poison—but only in gardens with no children and pets. Spread it on a piece of wood or stone near the nest, then cover for protection from rain. The foraging ants will love it.

A mash of hot chilies and water will keep ants away. Another homemade repellent is a mix of orange peels and water puréed in your blender and poured directly into an anthill early in the morning.

Ants hate aromatic plants like mint, lavender, chives, and garlic. Install these along borders or spot them randomly in clumps and pots around the garden. Create an ant barrier around plants, on front steps, and between garden rows with a sprinkling of agricultural lime, bonemeal, or powdered charcoal.

Fire ants, better known in the South as red ants, are especially partial to sun and sandy soil. If your yard is prone to infestation, provide shade with vine-covered trellises in a part of the garden where sun-loving plants won't be affected. And if you keep compost, store it in closed bins so that fire ants can't use it to build their hills.

APHIDS

Get rid of aphids the first time you see them; these pests reproduce rapidly. They not only suck the nutrients from a plant, but can also spread any number of deadly viruses, including bean mosaic virus and cucumber mosaic virus.

A simple and effective spray for aphids is 4 ounces of dishwashing liquid in 1 gallon of water. For another good spray, mix 1 tablespoon liquid soap and 1 cup vegetable oil, then add 2 teaspoons of the blend to a gallon of water—but don't use it on squash, cauliflower, or cabbage, which can suffer leaf burn. When using either recipe, spray the plants with the mixture and follow with a spray of water. Wait about fifteen minutes and repeat.

Sprinkle wood ashes over bushes and low-lying plants; they are caustic and will dehydrate and suffocate aphids. Use a large-hole shaker—the kind for grated cheese works well—or sprinkle them on by hand. After a day, wash away the ashes with a hose.

Praying mantises, ladybugs, and aphid lions (the larvae of green lacewings) are natural foes of the aphid. Obtain them from garden-supply stores and catalogs. Release ladybugs at night so that they won't fly away. Hoverflies and wasps kill aphids by injecting their eggs into them. Plant Queen Anne's lace to attract wasps and marigolds to attract hoverflies.

ARBORS

Tucked away in a secluded nook and sheltered by fragrant flowering vines, an arbor becomes a romantic hideaway. Set off by itself, it can accent the garden, offer an inviting destination, or command an imposing view. Arbors have utilitarian value as well. They provide shade in summer and serve as year-round screens for garden work areas, too. Traditional arbor plants include clematis, jasmine, wisteria, climbing roses, ivy, and, of course, grapes—a favorite since the time of ancient Rome.

A pergola is an arbor that you walk through. It can be a simple open framework or a series of arches that create a tunnel effect. Pergolas should have a focus—a destination, a view, or a path along a garden or across a lawn.

Design in proportion to the plantings your arbor will support. Anticipate the size of fully grown vines and climbers.

Delicate latticework cannot support mature wisteria, while heavy timbers will dwarf a fragile clematis. The best woods for arbors and pergolas are redwood, cedar, cypress, teak, oak, and locust. Use only heartwood, since sapwood will decompose rapidly. Pressure-treated lumber is an inexpensive alternative that is useful when lumber must be in contact with soil. It tends to bow and split, however, and doesn't take stain well. Pave the area beneath your arbor with brick, flagstone, or gravel if the arbor casts dense shade. Grass cannot survive without sunlight.

ARTICHOKES

Artichokes usually take more than 150 days to mature from seed and are highly sensitive to extremes of hot and cold. Coastal areas where temperatures don't fall much below 10°F and rarely go above 75°F are the best places to grow them. In areas with cool summers and deadly winters, however, you can grow artichokes as annuals—and take your chances.

To grow artichokes as annuals, soak the seeds for two days at the end of January, then mix with moist sphagnum moss. Refrigerate for four weeks in an unsealed plastic bag. When roots emerge, pot the clumps in 6-inch plastic pots of sterilized potting soil and place in a cool but sunny window. Two weeks or so before the predicted date of the last frost, harden off the seedlings by setting them outdoors in a cool but frost-free spot during the day. Plant in well-dug soil, spacing 3 feet apart, when all danger of frost has passed.

For tender artichokes, speed the growth of the buds by keeping the plants well watered. Mulch with compost or peat moss, and work some well-rotted manure into the soil.

If you grow them as perennials, get ready for winter by cutting off the large outer leaves and tying the center leaves together. Wrap in butcher paper and pile up sand, sawdust, or dead leaves as a protective screen against frost.

ASHES

Ward off slugs and snails by encircling your plants with a ring of ashes about 6 inches out from the stem. The soft-bodied creatures will turn the other way.

Your fireplace is a built-in source of garden fertilizer. Use the potash-rich ashes for most vegetables and flowers—except for acid lovers like azaleas and heathers. Store wood ashes in plastic garbage cans or heavy trash bags. Many of their nutrients—including potassium, phosphorus, and calcium—degrade rapidly when the ashes are moist. Fertilize with ashes a week or so before you plant. Spread 5 to 10 pounds of ash per 100 square feet over freshly cultivated soil or in furrows. Hoe in lightly. Don't mix ashes with manure or other nitrogenous materials, except for those already in the soil.

Make soil less acid by simply digging in wood ashes, which are strongly alkaline.

Heap a mound of wood ashes around the stumps of fragile plants like rhubarb, hardy fuchsias, and ferns to protect them in the winter. Rain effectively leaches nutrients from ash and supplies it to the root systems of the plants.

ASPARAGUS

Put in about twenty-five asparagus roots for each member of your family—more if you'll be canning. Allow 25 feet of row for every twelve plants, with the rows spaced 4 to 5 feet apart. If you can't plant immediately, keep the roots covered with damp sand or cloth.

If you're not sure the roots you've bought have been disinfected, soak them for fifteen minutes in a solution of 1 part household bleach to 3 parts water. Give them a good wash before planting to prevent the disease known as crown gall.

Plant each root about 8 inches deep—just enough for the crowns to be covered with an inch or two of soil. Place them 18 inches apart in the rows. Properly planted and maintained, an asparagus bed will yield a harvest for twenty years or longer. Just make sure the soil is rich in organic matter.

Mulch your asparagus bed every fall and spring to maintain a continuous 4- to 6-inch cover. Don't use sawdust or bark, both of which are too acidic. Asparagus likes a soil near neutral, or pH 6.5. Your autumn addition should include a 2- to 3-inch layer of manure as well.

Despite what you've heard, you don't have to wait until the second or third year to pick asparagus. The initial harvest should be limited to two to three weeks; add an extra week each year until the harvest is four to six weeks. Whatever the time period, stop harvesting when the average size of the spears declines to about the diameter of a pencil.

Cut off the tops in fall to prevent pests from overwintering.

AZALEAS

Azaleas and the other rhododendrons respond best to moderation in all aspects of cultivation: moderate light, moderate water, and moderate pruning.

Planting

Azaleas do best in mixed sunlight and partial shade but will blossom in full sunlight. Good drainage, acid soil, and plenty of organic matter are essential. To ensure proper soil conditions—especially in heavy clay soils—plant azaleas in raised beds. Alternatively, place the plant directly on a spaded-up surface, then mound up three or four wheelbarrows of a humus-soil mixture around and over the root-ball.

Don't fertilize when planting! The common practice of putting fertilizer directly in the bottom of a planting hole can be fatal to azaleas. Wait until the plant is established before you start feeding it. Use decayed bark or sawdust for humus. Don't use hardwood or fresh pine, which deplete soil nutrients.

Open the root-ball and spread it slightly before planting. When planting from containers, mutilate the root-ball by cutting or teasing it out. This will encourage the development of new roots.

A pH between 4.5 and 6.0 is necessary; 5.0 is ideal. If the soil is too acidic, correct with dolomitic limestone. If too alkaline, add iron sulfate or sulfur (don't use aluminum sulfate). Epsom salts can also be used to increase acidity. Scatter on soil at 1 pound per 300 square feet.

Azaleas like a 2-inch mulch of wood chips, pine needles, bark chips, salt hay, or oak leaves to keep roots cool and moist. But don't use peat moss; it seals in water and can promote root rot.

Maintenance

Fertilize sparingly. Azaleas often fall victim to too much fertilizer. For a good homemade fertilizer, combine 4 cups of dried coffee grounds with 1 cup bonemeal and 1 cup granite dust.

For rapid growth and dark green leaves, apply nitrogen in spring and early summer. Good sources are cottonseed meal, ammonium sulfate, manure tea, and urea formaldehyde.

Adequate moisture is critical for azaleas until they become established—at least two years after planting. Once mature, they can survive drought, although they're more susceptible to disease, insects, and cold. Wilted leaves are a sign of drought stress; water with a deep soaking.

Ease up your watering in the autumn. Watering induces new growth, which may not harden off before the first freeze.

Prune young plants lightly after they flower to promote lateral branching and a compact form. Remove larger branches from the interior of older plants to allow light in; sunlight inhibits disease. Cut away dead or diseased wood below the infected area.

Rejuvenate old plants by cutting the entire plant back to 6 to 8 inches from the ground. Or prune over a three-year period, cutting back a third of the branches each year. Prune in early spring, before new growth starts.

Disinfect tools thoroughly with alcohol or household bleach before and after using. And always complete pruning by early summer to avoid injuring flower buds.

Relocations. If an azalea outgrows its site, relocate it. Because of their shallow and fibrous roots, azaleas and other rhododendrons are among the easiest plants to move.

Signs of infection. Root rot and phytophthora are common fungus diseases of azaleas. Look for discolored stem tissue, branch dieback, and wilted foliage.

To rout fungus disease, cut out and burn diseased wood and spray the plant with a recommended fungicide. Sterilize the cutting tools afterward.

Insect pests. Yellowish speckling of upper leaf surfaces and black spots on the undersides indicate the presence of lace bugs or thrips. Get rid of them with an insecticidal soap spray or systemic insecticide. For whiteflies, use pyrethrum.

BAMBOO

Bamboos are not trees or bushes—they are grasses and grow as such. A shoot, or culm, forms in spring and reaches its mature height and thickness in the first year, although it will continue to branch out and add more foliage. If the plant is adequately watered and fed, each year's new culms will generally be bigger and taller than the previous year's.

Planting

Ensure success by planting container-grown specimens that won't risk transplant shock. Even though healthy plants are usually marked by sturdy, well-colored leaves, remember that you are really buying the roots, or rhizomes, where the future of the plant lies. As long as there are fresh young culms, the plant will grow and do well. Choose a sunny spot, sheltered from the wind if possible, in a rich soil that holds moisture. Don't plant bamboo in a waterlogged or boggy area, or the roots will rot.

This shallow-rooted plant needs room to spread out. Start with a hole twice the size of the root ball. In clay soil, dig an even larger area to loosen the soil. Soak the hole with water and let it drain before planting the root-ball. Backfill the hole with compost, well-rotted manure, or some aged manure. Soak again; finish backfilling the hole. The resulting mound should be slightly scooped and dish-shaped on top. Mulch. Water daily to ensure a good start and lessen transplant shock.

Maintenance

A good mulching aids in water retention, giving bamboo more top growth. Spread nitrogren-rich grass clippings around the plant in spring and summer. In the fall, spread a thick layer of leaves around the base of the plant to protect the shallow rhizomes from freezing. Use soaker hoses or drip irrigation to provide adequate moisture throughout the growing season.

Bamboo dies back in cold northern climates. But if you keep the roots well mulched, the plant will send up new foliage in the spring. In winter, don't worry about a heavy layer of snow— it is an effective insulator and will keep the plant from drying out over the winter.

Nutrient-rich compost and manure are the best fertilizers for bamboo, providing the valuable humus that also helps the soil retain water. In the spring, a handful of lawn fertilizer high in nitrogen is an excellent addition around each plant; just make sure not to use the weed-and-feed type. Sprinkle a handful of fertilizer after each rain until the new culms start to appear, and then don't fertilize again until the culms reach their full height and the branches and foliage are fully extended. At this point, a more balanced fertilizer is preferable. In early autumn, stop fertilizing altogether to allow the plant to harden off before winter sets in.

Unlike well-mannered clump bamboos, the invasive running types spread rapidly underground in search of food and water. Stop the sprawl one of three ways. One strategy is simply to encourage your plants to stay put by continually feeding and watering them. Another solution: In late summer, take a spade and sever any rhizomes the plant is sending out. Or you can contain the roots by erecting an impregnable barrier (polypropylene plastic, fiberglass panels, or rubber belting) set in a 16- to 20-inch trench. When the rhizomes reach the barrier and try to cross it, sever them or redirect them back inside.

Increase your grove by propagation. For clump bamboos, divide plants carefully into quarters or thirds. For the running types, take root cuttings of the outer rhizomes with their new shoots. Transplant immediately—without letting the roots dry out—at a depth identical with the parent plant. And be patient: Small bamboos take three to five years of cultivation to reach full size, while the giants can take ten to twelve.

BASIL

Sow seeds in March or April in a standard starter mix with 85 percent peat or a combination of 1 part compost to 1 part sand. Cover the flat with a piece of glass; it will act as a mini greenhouse, providing the high temperatures that basil seeds need to germinate quickly.

Don't rush to plant basil outdoors during the first spell of warm weather. This acutely cold-sensitive plant dislikes when the temperature drops below 45°F.

Pinching back the shoots ensures the growth of bushy, long-producing basil. Pinch plants just above the point where two side branches leave the stem. Don't allow flowers to develop; they sap energy from the plant's leaves.

Plant basil close to tomatoes. Folklore says these companion plants encourage better, stronger growth in each other.

BEANS

Beans like it hot. Sow bean plants only when the soil is very warm. Try this toe-tingling test: The soil is ready when you can walk barefoot in it without feeling the cold.

A chemical odor and a color on bean seeds—usually pink but sometimes blue or dusty white—lets you know they've been treated with a fungicide. Don't let children eat or handle them, and wash your hands after you've finished sowing the seeds. Better still, wear latex gloves.

Beans like company. If you take their pods away, they feel obliged to make more flowers—and thus more beans. Once in production, pole beans should be harvested every two days. This is less true for bush beans, which prefer to be picked only once or twice a week. Harvest beans young for maximum flavor and minimum toughness. Pick moist green pods that are tender and slightly filled out. Unless you're growing shelling beans, don't leave dried-out pods on the vines; they reduce the plant's production of new beans.

Never pick snap beans that are wet from dew or rain. Jostling a wet plant can spread the spores that cause one of the many mildews and blights that attack beans.

At the end of the season, cut off the foliage at ground level and leave the nitrogen-rich roots in the ground. Don't forget to rotate your vegetable crops annually to foil any diseases that are building up in the soil.

BEES

Bees are essential assets in any garden. In their search for nectar and pollen, they carry pollen from flower to flower, facilitating fertilization in many edible and ornamental plants. Attract bees to your garden by planting colorful, fragrant, nectar-rich plants; they're drawn in particular to contrasting colors, yellows, and anything on the violet end of the spectrum. But avoid planting tubular or trumpet-shaped flowers; bees don't like them, because it's hard to reach inside.

When you treat plants for insect pests, protect bees in one of two ways. First, never use an insecticide on plants while they are in bloom. Alternatively, control insect pests with *Bacillus thuringiensis* (Bt) or with insecticidal soap, both of which are harmless to bees. On melons and cucumbers, blossoms are open for only one day. Apply an insecticide in late afternoon or early evening, when the bees have returned to their hive.

BEETS

For an early harvest, start your beets in a cold frame in pots filled with garden soil. Transplant as soon as all danger of frost is past. Then protect them outside with a geotextile row cover. Early beets are tastiest when they're the size of golf balls.

Late varieties keep several months if you harvest before the first frost. Let the roots dry for a day outside, sheltered from the rain. Twist the leaves off and shake the soil from the roots. Have fresh-tasting beets on hand all winter by storing them in a root cellar or basement at a temperature of between 30° and 41°F. Place them in a case filled with sand or barely moist peat moss.

BEGONIAS

Learn to distinguish the three most common kinds: *Begonia × semperflorens* varieties are tender perennials that are grown from seed as annuals. They can be used in flower beds, window boxes, and pots. *Begonia × tuberhybrida* are tuberous begonias, whose bulbs are planted at the end of winter for summer bloom in flower beds or window boxes. *Rhizomatous begonias* include the famous *Begonia rex* and its hybrid offspring. These are usually propagated from leaf cuttings and cultivated as houseplants.

Begonia × semperflorens

Sow seeds by pressing them lightly into the soil, but not covering them. They are very fine and need plenty of light to germinate. Water the seed-starting mix from below to avoid disturbing the seeds. Do this by soaking the base of the flat in a larger container of water. When the surface of the mix is moist, remove the flat and let it drip before putting it back in a semishaded spot.

Wait until after the last frost to plant begonias. They can't stand the cold. If a late frost threatens, bring the begonia pots indoors for the evening and leave them in a cool room.

Darker foliage helps *semperflorens* begonias to tolerate more sun than those with lighter foliage. If you want to plant them in full sun, don't worry if some leaves scorch; they will fall off. The new set of leaves will be acclimatized to the greater light intensity, and your flowers will be all the more showy when grown in full sun. Remove all spent flowers and any leaves that turn yellow. An occasional pinching back will encourage your plants to be bushier and to flower more profusely.

Tuberous begonias

Don't skimp on the quality of the tubers. The bigger they are when you buy, the more flowers they'll produce. Take your pick

Planting tuberous begonias

1. Find the small point on the top; it will produce the stem.

2. Orient it toward the surface (note: the top is concave, which may confuse you). Start tubers indoors in February or March. Place side by side in trays filled with equal mixtures of sand and damp peat moss. Place the top end just under the soil, since many roots are produced at the tuber's rim.

3. If you can't identify the concave top, plant the tubers on their sides. The new shoots will grow their way up to the light at the surface.

of flower shapes: single and double blooms, either fringed or crenellated.

Plant the right way. See "Planting tuberous begonias" above.

For sunny locations, select the compact multiflora begonias, with single or double flowers. The other types prefer partial shade.

Keep it wet. The rooting medium should be moist and kept at about 70°F. When the shoots have two well-developed leaves, transplant tubers ½ inch below the soil surface, whether in pots or outside in the garden.

A few hours of sun in the early morning or late afternoon is to their liking. If grown in dense shade, begonias will grow tall and floppy and produce fewer flowers. Tuberhybrida types appreciate cool nights to recover from daytime heat. In areas where summer nights stay hot, they suffer.

Let the leaves yellow after blooming. The life cycle of this bulbous plant calls for a period of rest. Water less, but don't let the soil dry out completely.

Dry tubers thoroughly on racks covered with newspaper for a few days after lifting them. If not completely dry, they may rot. For winter storage, dust tubers with a fungicide, bury them in peat moss, and store them in a cool location (39° to 50°F), such as a porch, basement, or garage.

Rhizomatous begonias

Rhizomatous begonias are subject to root rot. Let their soil dry out completely between thorough waterings. And remember always to use water that is at room temperature.

Repot infrequently. Indoor begonias prefer tight quarters; rhizomes often overgrow the pot edge. Shallow pots are the best choice. To stave off powdery mildew, water early in the day and provide good air circulation around the pots.

Treat with a fungicide those species most sensitive to powdery mildew: *Begonia maculata*, *B. corallina* and its hybrids, and the semituberous *B. dregei*. Repeat the treatment every three weeks. Or spray foliage with a solution of 1 teaspoon baking soda added to 1 quart water. This changes the pH on the leaf surface, making it hostile to fungus.

To propagate from leaf cuttings see "Propagating rhizomatous begonias from leaf cuttings," next page.

Increasing humidity helps you to propagate successfully. Good containers include plastic sweater boxes with tight-fitting clear lids. Or you can simply place your cuttings in their containers inside sealed plastic bags. Make sure the plastic doesn't touch any of the cuttings.

Another way to start leaf cuttings is to cut the leaf into squares or triangles, each with a section of the main vein. Secure in soil by burying the bottom edge of each cutting in the potting mix. Plantlets will develop at the base of each leaf piece in four to six weeks.

Don't cut off the flower stalks of begonias chosen for their

Propagating rhizomatous begonias from leaf cuttings

1. Select a healthy leaf and cut off the stalk. Place it flat on a small board and cut through it in several places across the major veins.

2. Then place it directly on a tray of moist potting mix, with the top up, and keep it flat with a few stones. Plantlets will emerge at the incisions.

foliage. The pastel blooms, mostly white or pink, are a nice complement for the leaves. Remove the flowers when they die, however, to prevent seed formation.

BIENNIALS

Biennials are plants that live for two years. As a rule, they produce leaves the first year, then bloom, set seed, and die in their second year. Some biennials, however, such as pansies, are grown as annuals; others, such as foxglove and silver-dollar plant, self-sow so prolifically that they are often treated as perennials.

Planting

Plant biennial seeds in pots in early summer. Plant out in the fall at least six weeks before the first frost or overwinter them in a cold frame. Pinch out any buds that form the first winter to ensure bountiful blossoms the following spring. Don't let germinating seeds dry out. Fit the watering can with a fine-holed rosette so that the seeds are not dislodged by a flood of water. Or water seed flats from below by placing in a container of water until the mix appears moist.

For successful transplanting, water the seedlings before and after, even if the weather is damp. In dry weather, thoroughly water both the seedlings and the soil into which they'll be planted on the day before you transplant.

Biennials and bulbs marry nicely in the spring garden. In the late summer or early fall, plant low-growing biennials (wallflowers, stocks, and pansies) among tall-growing bulbs (tulips, daffodils, and hyacinths). Plant bulbs first; then intersperse them with biennials, following the recommended spacing guidelines. The bulbs will easily pop up, growing through a carpet of biennials. Lighten your workload by planting biennials that seed themselves. At the end of the season, allow a few plants to set and drop seed before pulling them up.

To avoid stripping your flower beds of blooms, site biennials for cut flowers in the vegetable garden instead. Biennials well suited to large-vase arrangements include Canterbury bells, foxgloves, stocks, and sweet william. English daisies make a charming little bouquet in a small vase or a medicine bottle.

In wildflower gardens, especially those in mild coastal areas, try growing the evening primrose. Harvest seeds from wild plants along roadsides, near beaches, and on vacant lots. The beautiful yellow flowers will bloom throughout the summer.

Maintenance

Deadhead hollyhocks at the base of the flower spike as soon as they are spent. This discourages seed-making and encourages reflowering the next season. Foxgloves should also be deadheaded at the base of the flower spike to encourage lateral shoots and another crop of flowers.

Protect windowsill pots of primroses and other flowering biennials from severe winter cold spells.

Cover them overnight with homemade cardboard or plastic covers, and remove during the day. Then continue nightly until the weather becomes warmer.

In chilly climates, place pots of young biennials such as wallflowers and stocks in a cold frame over the winter. Wait until the ground is workable in the spring to plant them out in a light, dry soil.

Grow the silver-dollar plant, prized for its use in dried arrangements, in partial shade in summer. Let the plant set and drop seed in the fall, then cut the stems. After the seedpods have dried out completely, rub the flat disks lightly between your fingers to remove the brown outer membranes. With luck and a bit of practice, the bright silvery central membrane will be left intact for use in winter floral displays.

BIOLOGICAL CONTROLS

Biological controls are any biologically derived agents that help control garden pests. For example, some insects, called beneficials, feed on destructive bugs: ladybugs eat aphids; green lacewings prey on a wide range of undesirable insects; and praying mantises will eat just about anything they can catch. Critters from bats to toads are also exemplary bug-zappers.

Ladybugs and other beneficials are drawn to nectar sources like Queen Anne's lace, lamb's quarters, and goldenrod. Other "attractive" flowers and herbs include members of the daisy family (such as yarrow), members of the carrot family (dill, parsley, and fennel), and members of the mint family.

Supplement existing populations of beneficials with commercially available ones. You can mail order ladybugs, lacewing eggs, and worms from suppliers around the country. A natural insecticide derived from a common plant grown in India, *Azadirachta indica*, arrests the development of various insect pests. It is sold under various names, including Neemix and BioNeem. Even nematodes are available; in many cases they can actually be helpful.

Be sure the beneficials visiting your garden have enough water to get them through a dry spell. Put out containers of water with rocks or sticks to act as perches. Change the water frequently to keep mosquitoes from using it as a hatchery.

Bacillus thuringiensis (sold as Bt, dipel, thuricide, or bioworm spray) controls cabbage worms and loopers, hornworms, and other damaging caterpillars. One of the most widely used and safest insecticides, it is available at most garden centers. Toads are among the most efficient insect eaters, but beware that they may consume as many beneficials as pests. Once you attract them to your garden, they'll need water and shelter. Sink pans filled with rocks and water into the soil. For shelter, simply place a broken flowerpot upside down in a shady spot.

BIRDS

Lure birds to your yard with a seed table placed in a wind-sheltered spot atop a solidly planted post. Fill with white millet seed to attract ground-feeding birds like doves and sparrows, or raisins for fruit-eating robins and bluebirds. Black-oil sunflower seeds are popular treats for chickadees and woodpeckers. Other easy table food: unsalted peanuts, whole-grain breads, cereal, and small pieces of apple, pear, grapefruit, and orange. Add a rodent guard to a feeder by placing an inverted cone, 36 inches in diameter, about halfway up the post. Or use a punctured metal or plastic garbage can lid.

Woo your favorite birds by building the houses of their dreams. Martins and swallows prefer apartment-style group houses. Wrens like sweet-smelling cedar homes. Bluebirds are drawn to lower houses—5 feet off the ground—set amid berry hedges. Place houses at least 200 feet apart, however, to keep the peace among these territorial birds. Supply your birds with little goodies with which they can build their nests. Tie onto a tree branch a plastic onion bag or meshed grapefruit netting filled with short string pieces, hair recovered from brushes, and snippets of scrap wool and cotton.

Birds will flock to your yard if you offer them a pool of their own, available year-round and preferably placed at ground level. It can be as simple as a garbage-can lid or a piece of plastic sunk into a depression. Birds don't like deep water, so fill the birdbath to no more than an inch or so. Clean birdbaths regularly. Birds use them for both bathing and drinking. Spread a little sand in the bottom for better traction.

Many birds love to roll in the dust. Indulge them by placing a flat container filled with fine dirt, clean sand, or wood ashes in a sunny spot near a bush or some other natural perch.

Birds feed, nest, and seek cover in such attractive and low-maintenance hedge plants as honeysuckle, blackberry, beech, yew, and hawthorn. Attract hummingbirds and orioles by offering a sugar-water solution. Use commercial feeders or try this homemade one: take a water bottle for hamsters, fill with sugar water, and suspend upside down. The mix should be 1 part sugar to 4 parts water. Woodpeckers love suet, but make sure that you put it out only in the cold-weather months; it becomes rancid above 70°F.

Don't deadhead seed heads on late-summer and autumn flowers like asters, sunflowers, cosmos, verbena, zinnias, and coreopsis. You'll be rewarded with the sweet sounds and colors of seed-loving birds dining in your backyard, even on the coldest winter days.

Many birds suffer an unsavory reputation as crop-devouring rogues. Some, like starlings and blackbirds, enjoy making mischief in cornfields and blueberry patches. To repel birds and stop them from feeding on fruit trees and crops, hang aluminum pie plates from the tree's branches or from sticks in the ground so that they swing about in the wind. Stationary objects—even scary ones like scarecrows and models of owls—

are eventually ignored by birds unless they are consistently moved around. Cover your plants with the protective netting designed to keep birds from getting to your ripening crop. Netting is available from most hardware and garden stores.

BLACKBERRIES

Enhance an archway or a split-rail fence with the lush foliage and pretty white flowers of blackberry plants.

Create a fan espalier to best see stems and fruit. In early spring, prune fruit-bearing stems to the ground. When the new green stems appear in summer, train them in a fan shape by fastening them with plastic ties to a grid or trellis.

Simplify pruning. On fan espaliers, tie all the sprouts from last year off to one side and concentrate the new sprouts on the opposite side. Don't forget to turn the young stems in the right direction as soon as they come out of the ground.

Prune annually after the final harvest. Cut to the ground any canes that bore fruit. Except for long, trailing types, pinch off the tips of young canes in summer once they reach 3 feet in height. Wear beekeeping gloves when pruning thorny blackberry plants. The glove's protective gauntlets should reach up to your elbows.

Thin the bushes just before spring growth begins, leaving only a half-dozen canes on each plant. Shorten side branches down to about 18 inches in length.

Plant a new patch every five to ten years, since cultivated blackberries pick up pests that lower productivity over time. Choose a new spot as far from the old site, and any wild brambles, as possible. Purchase only plants certified as virus- or disease-free.

BLEACH

Clean flowerpots before reusing by washing the pots in a solution of 2 tablespoons bleach and 1 quart water. Remove caked debris with a scrub brush or nail brush. Leave the pots to soak for an hour or more, then rinse and dry. You can sanitize garden pails in the same way.

Your pruning shears can easily spread virus and fungus diseases as you move from branch to branch and plant to plant. When removing branches that show obvious signs of disease—or have suddenly wilted for no apparent reason—dip the shears' blades into a bucket of undiluted bleach after each cut. Kill weeds and grass growing in sidewalk cracks by dousing with undiluted bleach.

BLUEBERRIES

Blueberries must have acidic soil (pH 4.5 to 5.0) that's well drained and rich in humus. Mix one or two bucketfuls of acidic peat moss with the soil in the planting hole. If your soil is alkaline, dig a hole 3 feet deep and 6 feet across and fill with a mix of 1 part peat moss to 1 part sand. To fertilize, use soybean meal, cottonseed meal, or ammonium sulfate—all highly acidic.

Oak leaves and other acidic mulches—including pine needles, wood chips, or sawdust—make blueberries thrive. Spread an inch or two over the ground beneath your bushes to protect the plant's shallow roots.

Birds love blueberries, and the only sure way to thwart them is with netting—from the top of the bush all the way down to ground level. When blueberries are ripening, a walk-in cage covered with netting can measurably increase your harvest. Support the netting with a frame made from plastic plumbing pipe, which can easily be taken apart when the harvest is over.

Low-bush blueberries make an attractive and productive ground cover. The plants grow only a foot high and blossom in spring with flowers resembling lilies of the valley. Leaves glow crimson in the fall. In winter the reddish stems bring a touch of color to the yard.

For superior taste, don't pick the berries as soon as they turn blue. Let them hang on the branches a few more days to develop the best flavor. Then "tickle" the bunches; the ripe fruits will fall into your hands. As long as you harvest all the good berries and clean up or cover with deep mulch any damaged fruits, your blueberry bushes should bear year after year with no disease problems.

Take special care to water regularly for the first year after planting. Give each new plant 2 gallons of water every week from the time growth begins in the spring until the end of August.

BOUGAINVILLEA

An unsurpassed climber in the subtropical areas of the country, bougainvillea is a striking covering for walls, pergolas, borders, and fences. It needs a strong trellis to support its heavy growth, and stems must be tied securely so that the plant's young shoots aren't damaged by wind.

In climates where frost is expected, shelter bougainvillea vines by planting them against a sunny, wind-protected wall. Or grow bougainvillea in containers and bring them inside during cold spells. Overwinter indoors in full sun and water just enough to keep the leaves from wilting.

Transplant with care. The bougainvillea's roots are especially intolerant of disturbance. When transplanting from a container to the ground, cut the container off the roots instead of pulling the plant from the pot.

Cultivars tend to flower continuously and are best grown where they experience no noticeable dry season. Feed and water your bougainvillea throughout the year.

BROCCOLI

Move broccoli to a new place in the vegetable garden at least every four years. Like other cabbage family members, it is subject to clubroot and cabbage worms; crop rotation foils both. This heavy feeder can also deplete the soil if planted in the same spot.

Cool weather is essential for broccoli. Make sure you time your planting to avoid the hottest months, since the plant will bolt in hot summer temperatures. Pack more broccoli into the same space by planting only 8 inches apart. Although the heads will be smaller, the total yield will be up to twice that of the recommended 18- to 24-inch spacing. Use plenty of compost, add lime to the soil, and rake in 1 pound of 5–10–10 fertilizer for every 25 feet of row.

When buying broccoli seeds, check to see whether the plant is a sprouting type. When the head of the main stalk on a nonsprouting plant is removed, no more lateral sprouts will form. A side-sprouting type, however, continues to produce new sprouts as you remove the developed heads. Always use an angled cut on the stalks so that rain or other moisture doesn't collect on the butt of the stem and set into motion a plant-killing rot.

Examine broccoli regularly to prevent it from flowering. Don't allow a single flower to go to seed.

BROMELIADS

Bromeliads that have a distinctive rosette or tubular shape, including the *Aechmea, Vriesea*, and *Billbergia* types, should be watered in the heart. In cool conditions, reduce the amount of water at the center of the rosette. Use a porous potting medium, not soil, and keep damp by misting. Plants of the *Tillandsia* type benefit greatly from weekly one-hour soakings underwater in a tub.

Encourage blooming by placing your bromeliad in a closed plastic bag with a few ripe apples or a ripening banana. The ethylene from ripening fruit will stimulate flower production.

Carefully remove the lateral offsets, or "pups," that the plant usually sprouts just before blooming. Although the parent plant eventually dies, these offsets will grow into new plants of the same kind. Remove the pups when they are one-third to one-half the parent's size. Plant in a porous medium at the level of the bulge in the base and stabilize with a stake. Keep the heart watered. Roots will form in about a month. Keep damp and out of the sun; misting helps.

BRUSSELS SPROUTS

In temperate zones, sow in mid- to late June and plant out in July, protecting small plants from heat. Sprouts will develop in the ideal conditions of fall.

Plants need a good 24 inches to produce well. Make use of the extra space by planting lettuces and radishes, which will happily grow to maturity in the gaps between the growing sprouts.

To make the sprouts develop at the same time, lop off the top 6 inches of the plant four to six weeks before your desired harvest date. Remove the lower leaves a few days before harvesting by snapping them sharply downward. This gives the sprouts more room. For the tastiest sprouts, harvest when they feel firm to the touch and measure from ½ inch to 1 ½ inches in diameter.

BUTTERFLIES

A butterfly house. Check garden centers and mail-order catalogs for the little wooden shelters that protect butterflies from birds and bad weather. Most come with a mounting pole, and all have narrow vertical doors that are too small for hungry birds to enter.

Showy displays of color attract butterflies. Plant flowers with blooms of vibrant purple, orange, yellow, and red. Single blooms provide better access to nectar than double blooms do. And avoid flowers that hang downward or have ruffled edges; butterflies will find them hard to sip from.

Plant in bunches. Butterflies are more likely to revisit a group than a single plant.

Overripe fruit is also attractive to butterflies. Leave dishes filled with mixes of mashed fruit, molasses, beer, or fruit juice in the yard. Or soak dish towels in the mix and drape them over trees and shrubs.

Certain plants are irresistible to butterflies. One is so attractive to the colorful little visitors that it shares their name: the butterfly bush (*Buddleia davidii*)—a graceful shrub with showy clumps of vibrant purple flowers. Marigolds, nasturtiums, impatiens, zinnias, hollyhocks, and daylilies are among the flowers they love, along with sweet william, heliotrope, purple coneflowers, bright red bee balm, and— not surprisingly—butterfly weed (*Asclepias tuberosa*). As for herbs, the most seductive are borage, dill, fennel, chives, and wild bergamot. Other good lures are wisteria, coreopsis, white clover, sweet alyssum, lantana, snakeroot, and sedum. Tailor-made seed combinations designed to attract butterflies are offered by some of the larger garden seed companies.

Remember that when you create an environment hospitable to butterflies, you're also inviting them to lay the eggs that will become caterpillars. The cabbage white, for instance, is a destructive pest to nasturtiums, cabbages, and radishes. One solution is to plant enough for both you and the pests. Luckily, most other caterpillars are not excessively greedy. At worst, they munch a few leaves without doing much damage—a small price to pay for the beautifully colored wings they will bring into your garden.

CABBAGE

Planting

Double your crop: Plant several varieties with different maturation times. In milder climates you can grow both spring and fall varieties. Start autumn seedlings in June and plant out in late June or early July. Transplant seedlings before the young cabbage sprouts its seventh leaf; the ideal number is between three and five leaves.

For more stable plants, bury them deep, sacrificing the bottom two leaves; new roots will develop from the buried portion.

Fertilize once a month, unless your soil is especially rich; your cabbage will mature faster and taste better. Scatter a 6-inch-wide band of 10–10–10 fertilizer around the base of each plant. Or if you choose, dress with some organic high-nitrogen fertilizer.

When planting any members of the *Brassica* genus—broccoli, brussels sprouts, cauliflower, collards, or kale—rotate the beds at least every four years to avoid exhausting the soil.

If you want small, tender cabbages, place the plants 8 to 10 inches apart. To raise bigger cabbages for stewing or stuffing, remove one out of every two plants to provide plenty of growing space for the remaining heads. Grow your plants in spring and fall to produce the most tender and savory cabbages. The summer sun tends to harden cabbage and make it flower.

Plant fall and winter cabbages around the periphery of your garden. This leaves the beds in the center free for a thorough end-of-season spading.

Maintenance

Cabbages have a tendency to split during hot spells or when moisture levels are erratic. If heavy rains follow a dry period while the heads are still forming, rotate each cabbage a quarter turn to break some of the roots. This slows water intake and inhibits splitting. Another way to deter splitting is to stop watering cabbages once they have formed a round head. Surround them with mulch or plant low-spreading flowers or vegetables between the heads.

Harvest a head by cutting about an inch above the soil. If you want smaller side heads to form, leave the lower leaves intact.

Drive away cabbage white butterflies, whose caterpillars love cabbage, by applying *Bacillus thuringiensis* (Bt). Spray plants as soon as the moths are noticed and continue every seven to ten days as long as they are visible, especially after a good rain. A spray of the plant's leaves is all that's necessary.

Fattening of a cabbage's root indicates the presence of clubroot disease, a serious problem with all brassicas. Pull up and burn all infected plants immediately. Adding wood ashes or lime to the soil for next year's crop is a fairly effective control. But the best way to eliminate clubroot is by not planting *brassicas* in the diseased portion of the garden plot for at least four to seven years.

Winter storage: Hang cabbages and their cousins, with their roots still attached, upside down in a root cellar, garage, or other cool place.

CACTI & SUCCULENTS

To make sure you're getting the exact cacti you want, learn their Latin names. Don't let Latin intimidate you, even if you're looking for the aptly named Texas rainbow (*Echinocereus pectinatus dasyacanthus*). Common names vary widely, even in the heart of cactus country.

Inspect plants at the nursery to make sure they're free of scale insects and soft spots. Note their stature: A plant that isn't standing straight in its pot is not well rooted.

Outdoor cacti and succulents are usually planted in raised beds covered with decorative gravel and surrounded by rocks or boulders—and with valid reason: Good drainage is essential. Fill the bed with a 50:50 mixture of soil and decomposed granite, pumice, or sand. Edge the bed with boulders placed close together and fill the crevices between them with concrete; the seams will be hidden once you fill the bed with soil.

Water cacti by drenching the soil and letting it dry out completely; it takes about a week. Succulents can tolerate more watering than cacti, even though they don't really need it. But they'll respond with lush growth if you water them daily when the temperature is above 90°F. Potted plants will need more water than those in the ground.

Whenever you need to move a large cactus, never drag it or roll it. Instead, grab it by the roots, loop a 6-foot section of old garden hose underneath, and lift with both hands. You'll need a helper for the heavier types.

CALADIUMS

These foliage plants offer a splash of color and pattern to any shade-filled spot in your garden. In the South, you'll often see them around the trunks of spreading shade trees. They also do well in patio containers and pots, with their veined leaves spilling out up to 2 feet across.

In May, buy dormant tubers and pot them in humus-rich potting soil with the tops of the tubers buried an inch deep. Carefully cut out the large main bud to encourage more shoots to form. Move the pots to a place where the temperature is 75° to 80°F. And keep the plants moist; otherwise, they'll go dormant. If you have a garden pool, pot tubers in porous terra-cotta pots. Once the plants have developed one or two leaves, place the pots on a ledge or cement blocks at the pool's edge, with the rims just above water level. The plants will respond with lush growth.

CAMELLIAS

This evergreen shrub, with dark green foliage and delicate blossoms, prefers a humid climate like that of the Southeast and parts of the West Coast as far north as Seattle. Plant in soil that is slightly acidic or neutral—never alkaline. Team them with acid-loving azaleas and rhododendrons.

Shelter the bush from frost, wind, and full sun. One favorite spot is the sun-dappled shade of a rangy evergreen. Mulch in spring and fall using a layer of well-aged compost about 6 inches thick. When the plant buds and flowers, apply ammonium sulfate at the rate of ¾ ounce per square yard every three weeks. Take care not to overfertilize.

Water the plants from above in midsummer; camellias thrive in high humidity. Encourage flower-bud formation by slowing down watering in September, moistening just the soil and using lime-free water.

Is it frost damaged? If your camellia has no leaves left, you have little chance of saving it. If there is only partial defoliation, prune severely above the healthy branches.

CARROTS

Planting

Sow seeds in a row or a band as thinly as possible—about three or four seeds per inch. Planting in rows is preferable, since it makes weeding easier. Tamp seeds with the back of a rake to bury them ¼ to ½ inch  deep. Thin out seedlings, leaving the strongest plant every 2 inches for small varieties and every 3 inches for larger varieties.

When you sow carrots, add a few radish seeds. The fast-germinating radishes will mark the row so that you'll know where to weed before the carrot seedlings emerge. Once the carrots are up, remove the radishes.

For straight, tender carrots, especially in heavily compacted soils, plant them in raised beds. Locate the beds in full sun, except in the hottest climates, where a little shade and extra watering are advisable.

Follow this rule when choosing varieties: The heavier the soil, the shorter the root should be. Varieties sold as either half-long or baby types are preferable to long, slim carrots for clayey, compacted soil. In extremely heavy soil, plant the round varieties, which won't have to penetrate as deeply.

Maintenance

To harvest sweeter carrots, apply a fertilizer rich in potash and poor in nitrogen. Too much nitrogen produces large, coarse, hairy roots that are devoid of good flavor.

Water seedbeds carefully. If watered heavily and allowed to dry out, the soil may form a crust that makes it hard for carrot seedlings to emerge. Water regularly and gently until the seedlings are established.

Control the carrot rust fly by covering beds with spun-bonded row covers immediately after sowing your seeds. In northern regions this remedy is necessary only for an early planting in spring. Otherwise, simply follow the old adage and wait until the apple trees bloom before planting carrots.

Varieties for home gardens sometimes have weak tops that break off at the collar as you harvest the root. To remedy, push the carrot into the ground a bit before pulling it out; this breaks the rootlets that hold it in the soil and allows the root to come free. Or stick a pitchfork into the soil parallel to the row 2 inches from the plant. Lean back slightly on the handle; repeat on the opposite side. This loosens even heavily compacted soil so that carrots slide out easily.

CATERPILLARS

Caterpillars can wreak havoc in the garden. Many home gardeners are reduced to trench-warfare tactics in battling these pests. Treat the problem safely and effectively with a bacterial insecticide that specifically targets caterpillars, such as *Bacillus thuringiensis* (Bt). Harmless to animals, humans, and most other insects, Bt controls cabbage worms and loopers, hornworms, fruit-tree pests, and other crop-damaging caterpillars. It is also effective against cankerworms, fall webworms, tent caterpillars, and gypsy moths.

To keep cabbage loopers from damaging cabbages and their kin, poke branches of fresh arborvitae or broom into the ground between the plants. Or spread tomato suckers on the cabbages after pinching them off growing plants; tomato foliage emits a strong odor that for a time will repel egg-laying white butterflies. Cedar shavings and chips also make an effective mulch that repels insects, snails, and slugs.

If a handful or two of your garden's cabbage loopers are chalky white and appear weak, your pests are infected with nuclear polyhedrosis virus (NPV). Put infected loopers in a blender with water and spray over crops. The remaining pests will die within three or four days.

The house wren, mockingbird, warbler, and catbird devour the larvae of harmful moths and butterfly caterpillars and numerous other tree- and shrub-attacking insect species. Install birdhouses in your garden or in nearby trees. Or erect seed tables and plant fruit-bearing hedges in the yard.

CAULIFLOWER

This "queen of the brassicas" is also the most sensitive to frost and heat. Choose the earliest varieties for spring planting. Better still, grow cauliflowers in fall. Start from seed in July; protect young plants from heat and keep watered. Plant starters as soon as possible after buying them at the nursery or growing them at home. Plant out in fertile, well-drained soil and enrich the earth once a month with a high-nitrogen fertilizer like manure tea.

Sunlight will quickly turn the creamy-white heart of a ripening cauliflower yellow or brown. Protect the heart—and retain flavor, too—by blanching (covering the head of a plant to block out light). Blanch in one of two ways: Once the curd has reached the size of an egg, break off a few outer leaves and place them on top of the heart, or simply fold the leaves over the heart and clip them together with a clothespin or rubber band.

Harvest cauliflowers before the curds start to separate— usually about two months after transplanting the seedlings.

CELERY

Celery is a demanding crop, requiring highly fertile soil, plenty of moisture, and cool temperatures to thrive. But time and patience may be the key requirements: Celery takes from five to six months to mature from seed. Start seeds eight to twelve weeks before the frost-free date in your region. Better still, buy transplants in flats, which are sold in garden centers around May. As satisfying as it is to bite into a perfectly crisp stalk fresh from the garden, don't overlook the varieties grown for the root (celeriac) or leaves.

If the soil is dry, grow celery in trenches 4 inches deep and 10 to 12 inches wide. Run a drip watering system or soaker hose in the trench to provide the cool, moist conditions that celery prefers. Digging compost into the soil before planting will help it retain moisture.

Soil too shallow or sandy? If so, plant celery in raised beds with amended soil to retain moisture and promote fertility. Be sure to water regularly, since raised beds have a tendency to dry out faster.

For tender white stalks, try blanching. Two weeks before harvest time, wrap the stalk cluster in cardboard or black plastic tied with string, leaving the leafy top exposed to the sun. Or cover the bottom two-thirds of each plant with straw.

CHILIES

Diverse and delicious, chili peppers are grown in much the same manner as sweet peppers but prefer slightly drier conditions. They can also be raised in containers to enliven a drab corner of the garden or the house.

The difference between chilies and other peppers is their level of capsaicin—the substance that makes them so fiery. Best known is the jalapeño, which has become standard American fare. A larger, milder pepper with more culinary uses is the poblano, called the ancho when dried. Other types include the tiny, searingly hot serrano and the spicy cayenne, which comes in both red and yellow. The cascabel is a small, round chili with brownish skin; dried, it sounds like a rattle when shaken. Seed catalogs often sell these and other chilies in seed mixtures.

To grow the hottest chilies, plant in the sunniest spot in your garden and harvest during the warmest weeks of summer. Keep in mind that southern gardeners should provide partial shade against the intense afternoon rays that may burn the pod. Northern gardeners should start chilies inside in pots to provide the long season required to ripen the fruits.

Plant chilies and their bell pepper cousins in separate areas of the garden. If cross-pollination occurs, sweet peppers may end up spicier than you'd like.

The best defense against chili burns on exposed skin is rubber gloves. Wear them whenever cutting or peeling a hot pepper. If the chili juice gets in your eyes, flush with water immediately.

Dividing clumps of chives

1. Dig up clumps that are 12 to 18 inches across.

2. Separate by hand or cut into pieces with a knife.

3. Fertilize and keep well watered. Pot extras and grow them indoor for winter use.

CHIVES

Chives are hardy and decorative. Use chives' blue-green foliage and pastel flowers to best effect along low borders in vegetable gardens or flower beds. Alternate with bellflowers or carnations for a pleasing look.

Divide clumps in early spring in temperate climates. In hot climates, wait until fall. See "Dividing clumps of chives" above.

The flowers that look so dainty in borders or beds ultimately hinder production and harvest of the leaves. Cut the flowers off at the base when they are buds and make little bouquets out of them; either use them fresh or hang upside down to dry.

Harvest often for maximum growth, cutting tufts about 2 inches from ground level. If the tufts are large, harvest only half the plant at any one time. To prevent yellowing, don't harvest the leaves in small bits. Use scissors or a knife to snip off whole stems or portions of tufts instead; this spurs the growth of new leaves. Your chives will remain tender and fragrant.

CHRYSANTHEMUMS

Get big, showy chrysanthemums simply by pinching off all the side shoots—the lateral buds at the top of the stems—between April and June as the plant grows. Keep only the terminal bud at the top. For best bloom, choose the varieties called florist's chrysanthemums, large-flowered mums, or football mums; plant between three and five per pot.

Train button mums or other small-flowered chrysanthemums to cascade over the sides of their pots by tying them to bamboo canes that are slanted progressively downward as the plants grow. In September, when the plants are ready to flower, remove the canes and let the plants hang down on their own.

Chrysanthemums as standards are possible with the most vigorous florist varieties. From early March, train to a single stem by removing all the side shoots and the basal leaves as they grow. When the plant reaches the desired height—about 2 feet—pinch out the top so that the branches of the crown can develop. Be sure you've retained enough of the higher side shoots to allow the top to form a full, lush crown. As the plant grows, maintain a balanced shape.

Many hardy perennial chrysanthemums boast a long and late flowering, even into November. They make colorful autumn companions for ornamental cabbage and kale. Look for them in catalogs under "garden mums." Pinch out the growing tips of garden mums regularly until about July 4 to encourage compact growth that will bloom heavily.

Shallow-rooted mums need extra winter protection to prevent heaving. After the first freeze, cut back the stems to ground level and mulch with about 3 or 4 inches of hay, straw, or shredded bark. This helps plants overwinter in temperatures as low as –10°F and escape the frost heaving that is caused by alternate freezing and thawing of the soil.

CLAY SOIL

If you spot spontaneous growth of buttercups, sorrel, thistles, or chicory, your soil is clayey. Another sign: if a puddle remains on the soil's surface after a rain. Still another: if the soil makes hard clods when dry and is sticky when wet.

Try double digging. If you're planting a vegetable garden, this technique is an especially good way to lighten and enrich the soil. See "Double digging clayey soil" below.

Another solution: Gypsum—calcium sulfate—is an excellent conditioner for clay, improving soil structure and aiding air and water penetration. Spread and work in 20 to 30 pounds of gypsum per 100 square feet for a new garden bed. For planting holes, dig a few spoonfuls into the bottom and mix a handful into the backfill.

Using peat moss helps to retain air and moisture. For every 100 square feet, use 9 cubic feet of peat and 20 pounds of lime.

Make your spading easier by puncturing clay soil with a pitchfork and wiggling it slightly as you withdraw it.

Large cracks are common in clay soil in summer, especially in the hottest southern states. Blanketing the soil with an

Double digging clayey soil

1. First dig a trench about 2 feet deep.

2. Add a good helping of compost or aged manure.

3. Then dig another trench alongside the first and shovel the turned earth back into the first trench, mixing it well with the compost.

organic mulch (leaves, compost, or pine straw) will enrich the soil with humus and keep it moist and crack-free. Replenish the mulch as often as necessary.

If you walk upon or till clay soil while it is still wet, you'll pack it even firmer. Instead, install permanent paths of brick or stone in garden beds to provide a place from which you can work.

CLEMATIS

Queen of the climbers, clematis is prized for its exceptionally long flowering period, variety of flower shapes and colors, and tolerance of almost any conditions and climate. Equipped with twining tendrils, the plant will attach itself and rapidly grow through thin-lathe trellises, bushes, and even other climbers. If you want to festoon a tree trunk or other wide support, first attach a piece of plastic-covered mesh so that the tendrils can grab hold.

Submerge the root ball of a nursery-bought plant in a bucket of water and keep it underwater until no more bubbles escape. Water the bottom of the planting hole (sited a foot or so away from the wall or support to allow for good air circulation) before planting. Fill in, firm the soil, and water thoroughly again.

Head in the sun, feet in the shade. The clematis grows best when its roots are kept cool and moist. Protect the roots with a thick layer of damp peat moss and straw. Or surround them with pieces of slate or roofing shingles or tiles laid flat. You can also keep roots cool by underplanting with any low-growing, shallow-rooted annual, perennial, or ground cover.

Let clematis cover—and beautify—a blank wall or fence by training it on a plastic-covered wire grid secured to the surface with nails. Note: plastic-covered wire is preferable to bare wire, which can often heat up and burn the plant. Position the wire at least ½ inch from the surface so that the tendrils have room to twine. For smaller wall spaces, a thin-lathe trellis makes a good support.

The best thin supports include a coated-wire or steel-tube arbor or trellis constructed from bamboo stakes, twigs, or wrought iron. The typical wooden trellis, with wide lathe lattice, is not suitable, since it necessitates tying the vine on with string or wire.

Plant two different varieties either in the same hole or side by side for a spectacular bicolored flowering. Or, to prolong the floral display, plant adjoining spring and summer species with different maturation times.

An evergreen hedge provides a good support for clematis, which offers in return a delicate, fanciful contrast. Allow the supporting plant to grow for two years before planting the vine at its feet. The clematis will then happily twine through its host.

Clematis that flower in spring do so on the previous year's ripened wood and require only light grooming. Late-blooming types flower on young wood produced the same year and require a hard annual pruning in late winter or early the next spring.

If the foliage of your clematis withers and dies from a girdling stem canker at the soil line, it's a victim of a common disease: clematis wilt. Remove and burn diseased stems, cutting well below the infected area. Sow new plants in a new location and grow in moist, neutral soil that is well drained.

COLD FRAMES

Often nothing more than a simple wooden box with the bottom taken out, a cold frame is an invaluable tool for starting seedlings, hardening off young plants, or storing bulbs.

Construct cold frames out of new or salvaged materials—bricks, wood, or metal. If you opt for wood, the pressure-treated type is the most durable. A slanted lid or roof made of glass, fiberglass, or plastic will maintain warmth inside and help seedlings and plants establish themselves. In winter, use canvas, black plastic, or other protective covers to keep out cold and snow.

Make a movable lid to be opened during the warmth of day and closed at night. Or fashion a prop that will allow the frame to be opened to different heights. An old window from a junk dealer makes a perfect cold-frame lid. Simply build the frame to match the window's dimensions.

Place the frame flat on the ground on well-drained soil. Place a layer of coarse sand or gravel on the bottom and top with good planting soil at least 6 inches thick. Height is important if the frame will be used for housing larger plants.

Provide your cold frame with periods of partial shade during the hottest days. A light sheer voile fabric, netting, or a straw mat makes a good summer shade cover. It also keeps rain, wind, and animals away from your flowers and vegetables. Keep a large cover securely in place by weighting its edges with bricks on the ground. For a neater look, simply glue a triangular piece of Velcro to each corner of the frame and sew matching Velcro pieces onto the fabric.

COMPOST

Packed with vital nutrients, compost is made by decomposing usable wastes in a pile or bin and then incorporating the finished product into the soil to improve its organic content. Fold the crumbly, sweet-smelling compost directly into the garden soil. Use as a mulch around trees and shrubs or to enrich houseplants. Or sift compost through a screen onto the lawn.

Build a compost bin from new or salvaged building materials, chicken wire, wooden pallets, cement blocks, or plastic. A garbage can makes a compact, manageable container. Even old refrigerator or oven racks can be put into service as sturdy compost walls. Whatever materials you use, be sure to build open slats or punch air holes to allow oxygen to enter and speed up the decomposition.

The wooden pallets used for carting make ideal organic building materials for your composter. Assemble them like cubes without tops or bottoms. Place the structure in an unobtrusive corner of your garden. Plan at least two compartments: one for new wastes, the other for churning rotted compost and for use. A luxury composter has a third bin to separate semiaged material from finished compost. Add boards to the front as the heap grows higher.

Improvise a lightweight compost container by using large, plastic potting-soil or garbage bags. Poke about twenty holes in the bag with scissors, fill with material, and tie off at the top. Leave the bag in the sun to allow heat to facilitate decomposition. Shake or turn the bag occasionally to mix. Bring the finished compost to the garden in a wheelbarrow and use right out of the bag.

Shredded or chopped materials decompose faster than bulky ones. Before you put materials into the compost bin, help the process along by chopping broccoli ends, apple cores, corncobs, citrus rinds, and other tough kitchen scraps with a sharp knife. Or use an old-fashioned meat grinder. Grind up branches, stems, and hedge prunings in a wood chipper, which can usually be rented from hardware or garden-supply stores. Or burn the wood and save the ashes to add to the heap.

While all animal products except eggshells should be avoided, many other throwaways work fine. Among the materials you might try are shellfish shells, wine corks, used matches, chewing gum, nutshells, and the cotton balls from medicine bottles. Pour vegetable cooking water, pickle and olive juice, water from cut-flower arrangements, and leftover coffee, tea, or broth into the compost heap instead of down the drain. Store kitchen scraps on their way to the compost heap in the freezer. In many cases (with lettuce and tomatoes, for example), freezing will even help speed up the decomposition process.

Layer the compost heap with a mix of materials to ensure rapid decomposition. Alternate layers of high-carbon matter like dead leaves, straw, hay, or wood chips with layers of high-nitrogen grass clippings, trimmings, manure, and meatless kitchen scraps. Add new matter to the hot center of the pile to speed breakdown and hide it from flies. And never put a large quantity of any one material in the bin.

If your compost doesn't heat up or is too dry, hose it down to achieve a damp consistency similar to that of a wrung-out sponge. If the compost pile is too damp, insert a few thin layers of an absorbent material; sawdust, peat, or cut hay all do the job well. To prevent the heap from getting too wet in rainy weather, place a layer of hay, dried grass, or a piece of old carpet atop the pile.

Turn compost materials regularly to provide oxygen for the organisms that induce decomposition. A pitchfork makes a perfect turning tool. If you're adding a big load to the composter, use a broom or rake handle to poke airholes in the pile.

Piles should smell sweet and fresh. A bad-smelling pile is your clue that compost is not getting enough air. To remedy the problem, incorporate dry, carbon-rich materials like dead leaves and sawdust, turning them into the pile thoroughly.

CORN

Corn will take up a good-sized chunk of space in your vegetable garden—not only because the plants grow large but also because you'll need numerous plants, since each 5- to 8-foot stalk will produce only one or two ears. Since corn is wind-pollinated, planting in blocks ensures that whichever way the wind blows, pollen from the male flowers (the plants' tassels) will reach the female flowers (the ears). Plant several rows so that each plant is more likely to be next to a plant that is in flower at the same time. The minimum for small gardens is sixteen corn plants, planted in four rows of four plants each.

To extend your harvest, sow three varieties with different maturities—sixty-five, seventy-five, and eighty-five days, for example—on the same day. Your corn crop should yield for two to three weeks, depending on the weather. Or plant one variety successively, sowing new seed each time the previously sown seedlings have grown four leaves tall.

When you plant corn, don't settle for conditions that are less than ideal. Wait until well after the last possible frost date, then listen to local weather forecasts or use a soil thermometer to make sure the soil temperature is 60°F or warmer.

Corn loves rich soil. Enrich the seedbed with compost, aged manure, and fertilizer before planting. When the plants are 1 to 2 feet tall, feed with a high-nitrogen fertilizer like manure tea or ammonium nitrate, sprinkling it beside the row.

Water the seedbed three or four days before planting and let it dry out to achieve the right moisture level. Watering freshly planted corn seeds directly will encourage rot in both seeds and seedlings.

Ears will be ready for harvest twenty or twenty-one days after the silk first emerges (exact time will vary, depending on the amount of heat the ears have absorbed through the summer). To check, look for silks dried to a dark brown. If still in doubt, slightly peel back the husk of an ear you suspect is ready, inspect the kernels, and puncture a kernel with a thumbnail; mature corn will ooze milky juice, not clear liquid. Once you become familiar with the way a ripe ear of corn looks, you can simply squeeze the tip of the ear to see if its time has come; it will feel plump and full.

The most effective prevention for earworms is a time-consuming one—but it's worth the effort to get a worm-free crop. A few days after the silk emerges from the developing ear, fill a medicine syringe with mineral oil and apply it to the base of the silk. Repeat the process every few days as the plant grows.

CUCUMBERS

Plant trellis cucumbers to save space and fight foliage diseases. Getting them up high improves air circulation and allows the leaves to dry more quickly. It also keeps them off the soil, where they are susceptible to rust and rot. Gravity may help trellised fruits grow straighter, but the plants will need more water because of increased exposure to wind and sun.

Sow your cucumbers in peat pots instead of flats; the delicate seedlings won't tolerate any disturbance of their roots. Sow seeds two weeks before the predicted date of the last frost. Plant them out when they have grown two or three true leaves. Set the plants out 1 foot apart down the center of a 3-foot-wide raised bed covered with black plastic mulch. Cover with a floating row cover. As plants begin to flower, remove the cover so that insects can pollinate the fruit.

Encourage branching by pruning young plants as soon as they are carrying four leaves. Pick off the top of the stem, leaving two leaves at the bottom. Grow better, stronger fruits by leaving only four fruits on a plant at the same time. When the tiny fruits begin to appear, thin them to four by picking them by hand; they'll pop off easily.

Don't allow any fruit on the plant to ripen completely; otherwise, you'll limit the production of new fruits. Always pick the fruits young. If the skins have developed a golden-yellow shading, you've harvested too late; by that time the cucumbers are overripe.

DAFFODILS

The daffodil is also known as the trumpet narcissus. It is distinguished from the myriad of other species of narcissus by the length of its central trumpet—as long as or longer than the surrounding petals. It comes in both single-petal and double-petal varieties.

Pinch off faded flowers with your fingernails or pruning shears, leaving the green stem in place. Removing the blooms speeds storage of the reserves the bulb needs in order to reflower next year.

When its leaves become yellow, the daffodil can become unsightly. But as with all spring-flowering bulbs, be careful not to lift them from the garden until their leaves fully ripen. To shield them from sight, interplant the bulbs with annuals and perennials, whose foliage will mask the daffodil's dying leaves.

Daylilies make fine companions because fading daffodil foliage will be neatly masked by daylilies' similar leaves. Other good screens are periwinkle and ferns.

DAHLIAS

For midsummer blooms, start dahlia tubers in early spring in a warm (at least 50°F), sunny place, such as a sunroom or conservatory. Place in a shallow box filled with lightly damp peat moss, sand, or leaf mold, which will let the shoots develop more easily.

Double your dahlias. When the shoots of tubers reach 6 to 7 inches, cut them an inch above the base and insert the cuttings in pots filled with a light mixture of damp sand and compost. Water and keep misted, or cover with a plastic bag and keep them away from sun. In three weeks they will root—and you'll have twice as many!

Larger dahlia varieties need a planting depth of 6 to 8 inches. Dwarf types need only 3 to 4 inches. Plant outside only after all danger of frost has passed.

To get big flowers, choose cactus- or decorative-type dahlias. Remove the weakest stems, leaving only two or three of the strongest, when the plants are about 4 inches tall; support with stakes. As soon as flower buds have formed, pinch them off or remove all the side shoots, leaving only the terminal bud. Water the plants well and feed regularly with a liquid 5–5–10 fertilizer.

For tall dahlia varieties, stake when the stems reach 18 to 20 inches high. Select three or four bamboo canes of the same height as the mature plant and drive them into the soil beside the main stems. Tie the stems at two heights with soft twine and incorporate the new growth as it develops.

Prolong flowering by deadheading your dahlias—systematically removing all faded flowers. So treated, the small-flowered dahlia varieties are capable of flowering for a full four months or longer without interruption.

DAYLILIES

The colorful bloom of the popular daylily lasts only one day—hence the origin of its name. Flower performance varies dramatically according to climate and conditions. A profuse bloomer in one climate may be a stubborn performer in another.

Look for two fans (young sprouts or ramets) when buying a clump. It means the plant is more mature, which will greatly increase the likelihood of bloom in the first season. Place plants at least 2 feet apart. In northern regions, set them out in spring. In warmer climates, plant in spring or fall.

Daylilies planted on a bank provide good erosion control. Their vigorous roots help hold the soil in place.

Plant red daylilies in a spot that gets relief from the hot afternoon sun, since these varieties tend to burn more easily than others. Or purchase plants advertised as "sunfast." Sunfast daylilies' petals are protected by a heavy, waxy coating that makes them more sun tolerant.

DELPHINIUMS

Delphiniums, which are also called larkspurs, are tall, stately perennials with lacily toothed foliage and towers of white, blue, or violet flowers. Mature height on some types can reach 7 feet.

Plant only in rich soil that is deep, friable, and well drained. Don't expect dazzling flowerings in dry, stony soil.

Delphiniums thrive especially in maritime climates; they're not suitable for the hot, humid, or arid summers of other regions.

Water their feet: Flood the root area until it is soaked. But don't spray overhead; getting the leaves wet encourages the spread of botrytis, a fungal disease to which delphiniums are particularly susceptible.

For blooms all season on established plants, simply pinch out the growing points of the outer stems early in the season to stimulate lateral growth. The central unpinched stems will bloom first, followed by the shorter outer ones.

Don't wait to stake. Do it as early as April. Only a few varieties—a handful of wild ones and small hybrids of delphinium belladonna—can stand without any support. An adequate stake must reach the base of the inflorescence, or floral axis, of the plant. Simple stakes suffice for low shapes, but medium-sized delphiniums need a special grow-through support. Place three canes around the plant and use string to create an outer ring and inner network. For the tallest delphiniums, make a cylinder of the required height using stakes encircled with a sheet of mesh or with string or wire. Or you can stake each stem individually with a bamboo cane.

Want a second crop? To enjoy a second flowering in September, cut back the stems of delphiniums as soon as the flowers have faded in June or July. Cut just above the basal leaves at a height of 4 to 9 inches. Water the plants copiously and apply liquid fertilizer several times throughout the course of the summer.

DILL

Plant this herb, with its wispy leaves and yellow blooms, in your flower border for a lacy background effect. If you decide to grow dill for the mature heads—which make wonderful fresh or dried material for flower arrangements—give the plants a foot of space all around, since they grow quite large. To use in arrangements, cut the head before the plant begins to brown. For dried arrangements or to harvest seed for flavoring, allow the heads to mature fully.

Plant among cabbage: The combined colors of dill and cabbage make a pretty picture. Dill's chartreuse-yellow flowers mix nicely with the blue-green of cabbage.

Let some dill flowers go to seed. Doing so will give you plenty of seedlings every year. Dill seedlings are easy to move.

Succession plantings can be made, but don't plant dill until after the danger of hard frost in spring—about a month before the frost-free date in your area. In warm regions, winter temperatures will rarely kill the plant, so you can plant in the fall.

EARTHWORMS

A garden filled with earthworms is a healthy garden. That's because earthworms turn raw organic materials into a rich manure called castings. These slender coils of fertile humus can often be found by the entrances to underground tunnels. Scoop up the nutritive castings and use in pots, planters, or window boxes.

Earthworms need nitrogen in their diet and will appreciate a supply of compost as much as your plants do. Never use synthetic nitrogen fertilizer, however; the salts will repel them.

To avoid cutting the worms up with your tiller, work in the middle of the day, when they burrow deep into the ground. When digging and planting, use a garden fork, not a spade. Contrary to popular belief, an earthworm that has been cut in half cannot regenerate.

Attract them with mulch, which provides them with food and keeps soil from becoming too hot and dry or too soggy and cold. Earthworms need an even temperature and moisture for their skin.

EGGPLANT

Buy established plants. Because seedlings need ten weeks of growth before transplanting and require the warmth of a greenhouse or other seed-starting arrangement, you'll be better off buying plants that are ready to be transplanted.

Make a depression at the foot of each plant to make watering easier. In cooler climates, space the plants 18 inches apart; in southern climates, space them 24 inches apart. Planting eggplants, tomatoes, and peppers together in their own corner of the plot makes crop rotation easier. Move them the next year to an area where no solanaceous plants have been grown for at least three years.

Pinching: In areas with long growing seasons, pinch with your fingernail above the fifth leaf when the plant has six or seven leaves. This spurs the lateral bud to bear flowers and fruit. Then pinch each shoot above the leaf that follows the second flower. In short-season areas, a single pinching will suffice. Each plant is capable of bearing eight to ten fruits for picking in late summer through early fall.

Put it in a sunny spot, where the soil stays warm. Eggplant is miserable in cold, wet weather and the darker, moister areas of your garden. In short-season areas, protect with row covers.

ENDIVE

Endive is part of the chicory family and comes in three forms: the leafy salad green known as curly endive, the broadleaf endive called escarole, and the crisp, blanched sprouts called Belgian endive or witloof. Among the other relatives are the fashionable red-leaved chicories known as radicchio.

Too much heat causes bitterness. In regions with hot summers, pick the spring crop of curly endive and escarole young, before the heat has a chance to ruin the taste. Better still, plant in late summer to mature in the shorter, cooler days of fall.

Grow as you would lettuce. Give curly endive and escarole a sunny spot in humus-rich soil. Try planting them among tomatoes to provide shade from the scorching midday sun. Also make sure the soil is well drained, since endive roots rot easily.

Like all chicories, curly endive and escarole have a slightly bitter taste. Mellow the hearts of the plants by tying up the outer leaves as they grow.

Blanch Belgian endive to produce the crisp, mild-tasting sprouts called chicons. Wait until the plant is two-thirds grown—usually about sixty days. Tie the outer leaves upright

Grow Belgian endive as a root crop

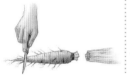

1. Sow about four months before the first hard frost date in your area (25°F or below) and thin seedlings 8 to 12 inches apart. If they form seed stalks, cut them down and allow the plants to regrow. Once frost threatens to freeze the crown, dig the roots. Cut the vegetation above the neck and trim the roots, leaving them 8 to 10 inches long.

2. Place the roots upright in a box filled with moist earth and store in a darkened room or cellar. Pour an inch or so of water into the container so that just the tips of the roots are wet.

3. Make sure that the root cellar or storage room is consistently cool (around 50° to 60°F) and has steady 90 to 95 percent humidity. You will harvest chicons in three to four weeks.

loosely with rubber bands. Untie after rainstorms to prevent rot and retie when the plant has dried. Blanching generally takes two to three weeks; harvest only on a day when the plants are dry.

Grow Belgian endive as a root crop in summer and take it inside for forcing during the winter months. See "Grow Belgian endive as a root crop," page 61.

To harvest from the forcing box, cut the heads with a sharp knife just above the top of the root. They will regrow two or three times, depending on the strength of the root and the quality of the care. Produce chicons over several months simply by leaving a portion of the roots in cold storage and forcing only a few at a time, as needed.

After harvesting, keep chicons cool and in total darkness. If you expose them to too much light before they're eaten, there is a good chance they will turn both hard and bitter.

FENNEL

As a culinary herb, fennel (*Foeniculum vulgare*) is grown for its licorice-flavored seeds—a prime ingredient in Italian sausage and curries—and for its leaves, used in salads and fish dishes. Another variety (*F. vulgare* var. *azoricum*) yields finocchio, also known as Florence fennel. This plant is raised for its bulbous leaf base, which is eaten raw or cooked.

Grow fennel in well-drained soil in a sunny location; in hot areas, provide partial shade. If conditions are right, fennel will self-sow readily, so watch for volunteers.

Fennel's lacy foliage and dainty flower heads make the herb handsome enough to deserve a spot among ornamentals. Mix it with roses and lavender, for example, or with any plant that has blue-green leaves, such as dianthus. While finocchio is half-hardy, a heat wave can cause it to bloom without forming a bulb. In the North, sow seeds indoors and set seedlings out two weeks before the last frost date; protect from late spring freezes. In the South, sow seeds in July to harvest bulbs in October.

For white, tender bulbs, cover the young plants up to their necks with soil when you bed them out; water regularly. Once the bulb begins to form, cover with more soil. Harvest after three weeks. In moist climates, take care that the bulbs don't rot.

FERNS

Planting

Shades of preference. Most hardy ferns prefer dappled rather than deep shade. The amount of sun a fern tolerates depends on the moisture content of the soil—the wetter the soil, the more sun-tolerant the fern.

Multiply your ferns. Collect spores for propagation by cutting off a healthy frond whose spores are just turning dark and drying it on a sheet of white paper. The spores will fall off and look like fine dust. Remove the frond and crease the paper to gather the spores for sowing.

Sow the spores by tapping the paper to sprinkle them in sterile soil in a sterile pot; mist lightly. Cover the pot with plastic wrap and stand it in a dish filled with a few inches of water. Set in a warm spot in indirect light and maintain the water level until the soil surface is covered with the tiny heart-shaped growths called prothalli—in six to twelve weeks. Gently lift them out and transplant them in a soilless mix; keep moist until they have developed fronds and can be planted out.

Dividing ferns. Dig up root clumps in early spring and, depending on their size, divide into two or three pieces with your hands or a spade. Make sure at least one growing tip, where new fronds are produced, is present on each division. Transplant and keep well watered until established.

Maintenance

Save time, save water. Each year at winter's end, mulch ferns with leaf mold or unfinished compost to keep soil cool and moist. Water ferns only during long dry spells.

Don't rake around ferns in spring or you'll damage the young fiddleheads; do your spring cleanup by hand instead. In fall, rake gently so as not to disturb the shallow roots. Let some leaves remain as mulch.

With most ferns, fertilization is not necessary. Simply add compost to the planting hole and spread more on every year. It will provide nutrients and improve the soil's water-retaining capacity as well.

Don't cut back in winter—the dry fronds of deciduous ferns protect the base of the plant. Once the new shoots show in spring, prune old fronds off at the soil line.

FERTILIZER

For healthy growth, all plants require three important chemical elements: nitrogen for vegetative growth, phosphorus for strong roots, and potassium for flower and fruit vigor. Plants need three other major nutrients—sulfur, calcium, and magnesium—as well as minute amounts of trace elements, including iron, manganese, zinc, iron, and copper.

Chemical fertilizers are made from inorganic compounds such as ammonium sulfate. Mineral fertilizers, like limestone, are mined from rock ground into powder or pellets. Organic fertilizers, including manure and bonemeal, are mostly derived from plant or animal matter. Fertilizer labels list nitrogen, phosphorus, and potassium by their chemical abbreviations: N, P, and K, always in that order. Labels also indicate the ratio of each element to the total mass. A 10–6–4 compound, for example, contains 10 percent nitrogen, 6 percent phosphorus, and 4 percent potassium.

What to choose? Do a soil test to determine the nutrient

Six ways to fertilize

Broadcast Spread evenly over soil; rake in if desired.	**Side-dress** Apply in a ring or line beside a plant or row.	**In holes** Work into the base of planting holes.	**Dig in** Spread over soil and incorporate fully.	**Top-dress** Sprinkle on the surface of a bed.	**Spray** Apply liquid food directly on foliage.

levels in the soil and watch for symptoms of nutrient deficiencies. Then select a fertilizer—either a simple or complete type—accordingly. Always follow the application rates recommended by the manufacturer. Using more fertilizer will not boost growth and may injure your plants. Some chemical fertilizers and fresh manures readily release so much nitrogen that they burn plants. Keep them away from seeds, seedlings, and foliage.

When to use: Plants vary in their requirements. Some, like herbs, need fertilizer infrequently; others, like roses, are hungry all the time. A rule of thumb is to feed most plants in early spring to stimulate growth but apply little or no fertilizer in fall so that top growth can harden off before winter.

With new beds, incorporate fertilizer when preparing the soil; simply broadcast it over the bed or row and dig it in thoroughly. For single specimens, such as shrubs, dig fertilizer into the planting holes or work it into the surface around plants. For established plantings, side-dress by scratching fertilizer into the soil beside the plants. In each case, water the fertilizer in well. Punch holes in the bottom of a 2-pound coffee can with a screwdriver to make a spreader for granular fertilizers.

Mechanical spreaders, either the drop or broadcast type, make short work of fertilizing large areas. Use only dry fertilizers to avoid clogs and messy cleanup. Make sure to keep the shutoff mechanism clean so that it can close completely.

With a drop spreader, apply fertilizer in a crisscross pattern for complete coverage, going horizontally and vertically over the same area. Use half the recommended spread rate in each direction. Station fertilizer bags around the area where you're working. When it's time to refill the spreader hopper, it will save you a long walk.

FUNGICIDES

To pick the proper fungicide, find out exactly what kind of fungus disease is attacking your plant. Among the most common culprits are verticillium wilt, fusarium wilt, clubroot, botrytis, powdery mildew, and rusts. Your local garden center, nursery, or Cooperative Extension Service can help identify the disease and suggest the safest and most effective method of control.

To work effectively, many fungicides must be applied before a disease starts to develop. Note which plants in your garden are attacked by fungus each year and use a protective agent before any trouble begins. Sometimes a problem you suspect is fungal disease is actually the result of overwatering, underwatering, or a nutritional imbalance in the soil. If so, a fungicide will be of absolutely no benefit. Seek expert advice when in doubt.

How to spray: Treat all leaf surfaces thoroughly, even on the undersides, and work your way up carefully from the lower leaves to the top of the plant. But apply the fungicide sparingly:

An overdose can kill a plant. Read the manufacturer's directions and follow them to the letter.

Painting or spraying leaves with a mixture of 1 teaspoon baking soda and several drops of vegetable oil dissolved in a quart of water helps control powdery mildew on houseplants and cucurbit crops. On roses it protects against both powdery mildew and black spot.

Limiting fungicide use

Many types of plants have been bred to resist fungus diseases. Choose disease-resistant plants; plant catalogs should indicate any resistance bred into their products; if you are unsure, call and ask before ordering.

When sowing seeds indoors, use sterilized potting media or seed-starting mix to avoid damping-off disease, which affects seedlings.

Plant annuals and perennials far enough apart and away from hedges and buildings to allow good air circulation.

Rotate each crop's location in the vegetable garden every year to stay one step ahead of any soil-borne diseases.

Rake up all fallen leaves and fruit infected with fungi from around plants, and dispose of them to reduce disease problems in the future.

Water your plants early in the day so that the foliage will dry completely before the dampness of evening returns.

GARDENIAS

Gardenias love the South, thriving in hot, humid summers and mild winters. They are usually grown as border shrubs and hedges—especially close to the house, where the fragrance of their cream-colored flowers can be enjoyed by those indoors. In the North, gardenias are usually grown indoors, where they decorate sunrooms and conservatories. To keep them from dropping their leaves and buds, give them plenty of light and humidity. Put them on a tray filled with pebbles and an inch of water. But don't allow plants to get overheated, since new buds won't set in temperatures above 60°F. In summer you can move them outdoors to a lightly shaded spot.

To thrive, gardenias must have moist, acid soil enriched with plenty of organic matter. Although gardenias need warmth and sun, whether growing indoors or out, they also appreciate having their foliage sprayed with cool water early in the day.

Don't use a vase. Because the stems of cut gardenias don't take up water well, the delicate flowers are best displayed floating in a shallow bowl. Handle them gently to avoid bruising the petals.

GARLIC

Planting

Buy bulbs from catalogs or garden centers. Don't use garlic from the grocer, which has been adapted for commercial production. The best time is around mid-October, so that cloves can establish a good root system that will withstand heaving.

For maximum production, plant only the biggest cloves from the outside of the largest bulbs; eat the culls and the runts. Plant in full sun, in rich, well-drained soil. Rotate every two years to prevent lower production and crop damage from soilborne diseases.

Maintenance

Garlic likes evenly moist soil, so water well until the tops die back. Mulch to prevent drying and bolting.

Knot the stems, if you like, at the end of the season before the harvest. This helps the stems to dry out more quickly and is thought to concentrate more potent juice in the cloves.

Reader's Digest Quintessential Guide

Harvest

Pull your garlic once three-quarters of the stems become dry and brown. Leave the crop in the sun for a day or two, then move it to a dark, dry place to finish curing for a week. Trim off the tops and store the heads in mesh bags at 40° to 50°F in relatively low humidity. Never keep garlic in a moist root cellar; it will rot there.

GERANIUMS

Purchasing

The popular annuals and tender perennials sold in garden centers vary in price and quality. Generally, geraniums grown from seed are of less value. Those raised from cuttings perform better but cost more; they're also sold by variety rather than color. Before you choose a plant, ask the staff which types they sell.

Buy potted geraniums in the early spring. Look for bushy, well-rooted plants with one or two blooms so that you can be certain of their color. Single-flowered geraniums and those with darker leaves will grow better than double-flowered varieties in areas that have few sunny days.

Planting

Avoid big pots. Large, roomy pots encourage geraniums to produce a profusion of leaves instead of a profusion of flowers. Use medium-sized pots instead.

Grow varieties from seed if you choose not to keep your geraniums from one year to the next. Start them in flats on top of a radiator or another warm spot in January for flowers by early June. Four to six weeks after they sprout, transplant the seedlings to medium-sized pots and keep them in a cool but sunny spot. Move your plants outside in April or May, depending on your region's last frost date.

Propagate geraniums from cuttings

1. Take a healthy stem—preferably one with no flowers. Strip off the stipules and cut the stem into several sections.

2. Make sure that each section has a leaf joint and one to three leaves; remove any flowers or buds.

3. Dry the cuttings for about six hours, then dip the bottoms of each in rooting hormone and bury about halfway down in damp sand or well-drained potting soil.

4. The stem sections should send out roots and be ready for transplanting to pots or window boxes in about four weeks. Mist lightly or cover the plants with large plastic bags to help increase the humidity around them.

Propagate from cuttings in late spring or early summer. See "Propagate geraniums from cuttings" above.

Maintenance

For more flowers, pinch back the stems of your newly purchased plants. More branches will grow, with each bearing flowers by summer. Pinch regularly, and you'll be rewarded with blooms right up to the first frost of fall.

Don't overwater. It causes root rot, especially if drainage is poor. With deeper pots you may need to water only once a week. Add fertilizer to the water, using a tenth of the recommended dose; applying small amounts of fertilizer often is preferable to larger infrequent doses. Don't mist or sprinkle. Moisture on the flowers may cause them to rot.

Deadhead faded blooms. Snap or pinch them off by hand to prevent the plant from going to seed and to keep it looking nice and tidy.

If rust spots appear on the leaves, water the plant thoroughly, place it in a plastic bag, and set it outdoors in full sun. Rust-causing fungi will die at 90°F, which will be reached quickly in the bag. But beware: Don't leave the plant in the bag for more than a few hours.

Storing

To keep potted plants from one year to the next, bring them inside. Put them in a sunny, well-ventilated room and reduce watering. Give each plant 8 ounces of water every two weeks and turn the pots regularly for balanced growth. In early spring, start watering plants more frequently and cut back any scraggly stems.

If your basement is damp, try hanging geranium plants upside down there, wrapped in newspaper; if they're left on the ground, they'll rot. Space them well apart to allow for air circulation.

GLADIOLUS

For an extended floral display, plant corms in full sun as soon as possible after the last frost. Then plant every two weeks, continuing until two months before the first frost is predicted.

Don't plant in rows. Add gladiolus to a mixed bed, where their long stems will enjoy the shelter provided by surrounding plants. As a bonus, they will flower a few weeks earlier than those in an isolated bed. To keep the top-heavy flower spikes from pulling out of the ground in sandy soil or on windy days, plant the corms between 3 and 8 inches deep, depending on their size. Promote drainage by placing a layer of sharp sand or organic matter in the bottom of the planting hole. Press corms in firmly.

Stake large-flowered gladiolus, which can grow 4 to 6 feet tall, with a bamboo cane and soft twine. Place the stake behind the flower spike as soon as you can tell which way the florets will be facing.

Gladiolus florets open from the lower part of the stem upward. Pinch out the top bud to speed the opening of flowers all along the spike.

Dig corms when the leaves begin to turn yellow—about six weeks after bloom. Lift the plants carefully with a spade, shake off the soil, and set them aside to dry for a few days. Then cut the leaves to 2 inches before storing the corms in a cool, dry place.

GRAPEVINES

Planting

European grapes are most often grown in the long warm-season parts of the West, while American species will grow in short-season areas. A third kind, muscadine, is best suited to the South.

Plant vines in early spring or fall in a well-weeded, well-drained site amended with plenty of organic matter; they prefer a soil pH of around 6.0. Soak the roots in manure tea or in water mixed with a little bonemeal for thirty minutes before planting. Space vines 8 feet apart. If you plant in fall in a cold area, mound up the soil to prevent frost heaving. To ensure that fruits develop a high sugar content, plant the vines where they'll receive the maximum sun and heat. Site vines against a

wall or on a slope with a southern exposure. A vine-covered pergola over a deck or patio provides shade in summer. Keep in mind, though, that birds will peck unprotected fruit, which may then attract wasps and bees.

Quick propagation: In autumn, take 8-inch sections of vine, cutting just above and below a node. Bury two-thirds of their length in well-drained soil

Reader's Digest Quintessential Guide

or sand. To protect from cold, cover the exposed third with a mound of sand until the next spring. Transplant the cuttings in autumn.

Maintenance

An easy and tidy way to grow grapes on a pergola is to train a single, permanent stem—called a cordon—overhead, along the length of the structure. Fruiting canes will grow perpendicular from the cordon. Prune any canes less than a foot apart back to the cordon. Each winter, prune all canes down to two buds.

Prune a grapevine anytime it is leafless. In areas with hard winters, wait until just before growth begins in spring so that you can recognize and remove any dead or damaged wood.

Bleeding vines? Don't worry. Grapevines naturally bleed profusely when they are pruned in spring—but are not harmed.

Mulch in spring to give grapevines the moisture they need for good production. For best results, use plenty of well-rotted manure mixed with straw.

Grapevines quickly exhaust the soil. Side-dress each vine in spring with a 6-inch ring of a complete or high-potassium fertilizer. You can also add a pound of compost per foot of row in late winter each year.

Protect fruit clusters from diseases, insects, and birds as soon as the grapes reach the size of a pea. Slip specially made bags of transparent paper or cheesecloth up to the stem and secure loosely. If you use plastic bags, punch holes for ventilation.

GREENS

Greens comprise a range of vegetables grown for their leafy, dark green tops—each one distinctive and flavorful. Pick from collards, kale, broccoli rabe, or turnip, mustard, and beet greens.

Make a rich bed by turning rotted manure or compost into the ground as soon as it can be worked. Add 1 to 2 pounds of 10–10–10 fertilizer for every 50 square feet. Kale and collards prefer soil with a pH of 6.5 or above, so amend accordingly.

Fertilize again for maximum production of nutritious leaves and stems. Feed greens when they are about 6 inches tall by spreading a band of 10–10–10 fertilizer at the rate of 1 cup per 10-foot row.

Vary your crop. To ensure a ready supply, plant a short row of the greens of your choice every ten days in spring and summer. A staggered planting scheme means you can always harvest the leaves in their prime.

Harvest them young. Cut turnip greens and mustard greens while they're still young and tender. For tasty beet greens, harvest when the beets reach the size of marbles. Use greens immediately after picking them for the best taste.

Don't till kale under in fall. Let it grow through winter to be enjoyed as a fresh vegetable treat. If the leaves are frozen, don't thaw them before steaming or boiling. Some gardeners say that kale, as well as collards, tastes sweeter after the first frost.

Collard greens, usually grown in fall and winter, stand up well to heat. Planted in spring, they can make it through even the hottest months.

A turnip variety developed for its tender greens is called "all top hybrid." For tasty beet greens, grow the heirloom beet 'Chiogga'. Collards lovers praise the flavor of 'Vates', while experienced kale growers swear by 'Russian Red', also known as 'Rugged Jack'. For the fastest-growing mustard greens, choose 'Tendergreen'.

HEATH & HEATHER

Heath *(Erica spp.)* and heather (*Calluna vulgaris,* with its many cultivars) are low-growing subshrubs that offer an array of foliage and flower colors. Leaves may be green, gold, bronze, or silver-gray, and the bell-like blooms run from ivory to lilac to carmine. It's possible to have heath and heather blooming in the garden throughout the year. Choose varieties according to their flowering period.

Heath and heather look best when planted in drifts by themselves. Mass the plants in large swatches with complementary foliage or flower colors; use at least five plants of each variety and space at intervals of 12 to 18 inches. In a few seasons, the ground will be covered with a colorful patchwork. Spread an acidic mulch like pine bark or pine needles and keep the beds weed-free until the plants fill in.

Heath and heather prefer a light, quick-draining soil that is slightly acidic—with a pH of 6.0 to 6.5. If your soil isn't suitable, set the plants in raised beds filled with leaf mold, peat moss, and sand.

Plant heath and heather in full sun. In shade they bloom sparsely and tend to become leggy. Use the plants in rock gardens or as a "carpet" spreading before a conifer hedge. Accent them judiciously with dwarf conifers and azaleas.

Prepare a hole at least twice the width of the root-ball but only deep enough to accommodate the shallow roots; the plant should "sit" in the soil at the same depth it did in the nursery pot. Backfill with soil amended with compost, peat, or sand. Scoring—lightly slashing the root-ball in two or three places—often helps heather become established more quickly.

Prune after flowering to stimulate growth and help plants retain their compact, cushiony shape. But don't shear them into tidy mounds—they are slightly wild and "spiky" by nature. Cut back the stems just below the blooms. If pruning in fall, make sure plants have time to harden off before cold weather sets in.

While the plants hate wet feet, they love moisture. Never let them dry out, especially when young, and water deeply as needed when it's hot.

HERBS

Growing an herb garden isn't difficult. Most herbs are hardy, pest- and disease-resistant, and not too fussy about soil. First choose a sunny spot—most herbs do best with five to six hours of sun a day. It can be a corner of the vegetable garden or the border of your flower bed. Or create a new space just for herbs; if it's near the kitchen door, all the better. The design can be as elaborate as a traditional knot garden or merely a random mixture.

Not all herbs are grown just for their flavor. Many, such as rosemary, thyme, and sweet bay, are also valued for the scents they give to potpourri and herbal wreaths. Others, like chamomile and ginger, have traditional medicinal as well as culinary uses. Some herbs with prominent flowers—dill and lovage, for example—make beautiful, fragrant bouquets to put in a guest's room or take to a friend.

The right time for picking: Harvest flowers as soon as they blossom and are still only half open. Harvest stems and leaves just before the plant flowers, when herbs' essential oils are strongest. Harvest seeds when they have hardened slightly. Pick flowers, leaves, seeds, and stems only from healthy plants that haven't been sprayed with pesticides. Don't take damp plants, which can become moldy. Pick in the morning, after the dew has dried. You can also harvest in late afternoon. But remember that the sun's heat causes the amount of essential oils—the herb's source of flavor—to lessen. Before drying herbs or using them fresh, sort out and discard any damaged pieces.

HIBISCUS

Even if you live in a cool climate, you may be able to find hibiscus in the spring at a nursery or garden center. Once the weather warms, plant young specimens in a sunny location and treat as an annual. They'll flourish until the first frost, providing months of flowers that beautifully evoke the tropics.

The lovely Chinese hibiscus (*Hibiscus rosa-sinensis*) is perhaps the best-known species, although it is hardy only in the warmest areas: Florida, the Gulf Coast, California, and Hawaii. It is prized for its large, disklike blooms of white, yellow, pink, and red. Gardeners in cold climates can enjoy *H. syriacus*, a shrub known as althea or rose of Sharon. Another is rose mallow (*H. moscheutos*), a wetland plant with flower cups up to 12 inches across.

To plant in containers, put each hibiscus in a 2- to 5-gallon pot. Place outdoors in a warm, sunny spot after the danger of frost has passed. To maintain deep green leaves and vibrant flowers where summers are torrid, provide some filtered shade.

When night temperatures drop below 50°F, move potted hibiscus indoors by a sunny window. Be careful not to overwater in this dormant phase; let the top inch of soil dry out before watering.

HOEING

Hoe before a rain. Hoe hard, crusted soil before a summer downpour. Instead of running off quickly and eroding the topsoil, the rainwater will be able to penetrate deeply below the surface.

Don't hoe during a drought. While hoeing to uproot weeds, you expose more soil to the air, which lets more moisture evaporate. Combat weeds instead by spreading a water-retentive organic mulch.

Hoe in the dark. Discourage light-sensitive weed seeds from germinating by cultivating the soil after sundown.

Use a hoe with a handle at least 4 feet long so that you can work standing straight—not bent over, straining the back. Keep the blade sharp and slide it below but parallel to the surface to loosen clods and sever weed roots.

For delicate work, many types of small hoes are available, including heart-shaped, rectangular, or three-pronged ones.

These narrow tools will penetrate everywhere and can be used between flowers and vegetables without the usual risk of bruising.

Should you hoe in winter? Yes, if the ground isn't frozen. Cold-weather hoeing gives you the chance to destroy grubs, cutworms, and other soil-dwelling pests.

One weed not to hoe is common purslane, a ground-hugging annual pest. Its tiny seeds remain in the soil and germinate if exposed by cultivation, and its fleshy, water-retaining stems can form new roots even after the plants are hoed up. Pull out seedlings by hand or treat with herbicides.

HOLLY

Climate is an important consideration when choosing hollies. Chinese holly and yaupon holly thrive in warm areas, while American and Japanese hollies are better suited to temperate zones. For the cold northern states, choose the inkberry or winterberry types.

If the sharp spines of holly leaves bother you, select a variety that has either no spines or only a few on each leaf. These include Chinese holly, Japanese holly, and longstalk holly. For profuse red berries, use both male and female plants. Only female specimens will produce berries—and only when pollinated by a male.

In cold climates with windy winters, plant hollies in sheltered areas to prevent leaf damage. Further protect plants by spraying in the fall and winter with an antidesiccant—a substance that keeps the leaves from losing moisture.

Not all hollies are evergreen. Winterberry hollies drop their leaves in the fall but compensate with a profusion of bright red, orange, or yellow berries all winter. In addition to providing spectacular color in a drab season, they are tolerant of wet soil and partial shade—and adapt to almost all parts of the country.

HORSERADISH

To prevent forked roots, grow horseradishes in drainage-pipe sections placed vertically in the ground and filled with a rich soil mixture. Roots will grow straight and thick until fall harvest.

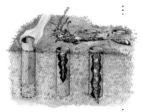

Horseradish leaves are known to have fungus-fighting properties—especially against brown rot, which attacks fruit trees. Mash the leaves to extract their juice, strain, and spray on plants.

HOSTA

These hardy perennials, prized more for their large, beautiful leaves than their trumpetlike flowers, are mainstays for shady borders and pond sides. They are also effective as a ground cover.

Hostas are sun shy; the large leaves they produce to collect light will scorch if overexposed. Select their site with care, noting the amount of sun a prospective planting site receives before setting them out. In cool climates hostas can tolerate about four hours of sun daily; in warm climates, an hour of direct sun is the limit. Keep them well watered.

Hostas are notorious for attracting slugs and snails. To thwart them, try growing the plants in wooden containers encircled with copper tape—which slugs are reluctant to cross. The tape is available through garden-supply companies; simply staple several strips all the way around the container. Lessen slug damage by keeping the plant's bed free of weeds and decomposing leaves. The improved growing conditions will not only strengthen the plants but also deprive the pests of nesting sites and make it easier to detect and destroy eggs and adults.

While hostas are adaptable, easy-care plants, they will thrive for years if given rich soil and plenty of moisture. Because hostas need a period of dormancy, they grow well where the temperature drops below freezing for two to three months of the year.

To fill in spaces between hostas while they mature, plant impatiens, which share the same cultural conditions and will self-seed for a few years as hostas reach full size.

The bold, sculptural leaves of *Hosta sieboldiana* make a perfect foil for ferns and arrow bamboo (*Pseudosasa japonica*).

Multiply by division. For more hostas, divide mature root clumps in early spring or in fall, after the leaves have died back.

HUMMINGBIRDS

Like bees, hummingbirds pollinate your garden. An extra bonus is that they're delightful to look at. Build a trellis for trumpet creeper, morning glories, and honeysuckle. When the vines bloom, hummingbirds will arrive.

Hummingbirds like flowers that are red, orange, and bright yellow. Bee balm, zinnia, salvia, daylily, penstemon, and red-hot poker are good choices.

To create a simple feeder, cut a red plastic plate in the shape of a hibiscus flower. Fill a hamster water bottle with sugar water tinted with red food coloring and insert it into the center of the "flower," securing it on the back with duct tape. Hang amid the flowers on your trellis or rhododendrons, whose blooms attract the birds. Even after the flowers fade, the birds will keep coming back.

HYACINTHS

While hyacinths herald spring's arrival in the garden, you can enjoy them indoors in winter by forcing bloom. Plant bulbs with their "shoulders" exposed in a moist, well-drained potting mix and store at 40°F for twelve to fifteen weeks before desired bloom time. To break their dormancy, move them to a warm (55° to 65°F), bright, but not sunny, spot until sprouts appear, then place in direct sun; keep well watered. Once buds show color, put plants in indirect light, which will help prolong flowering. Blooms will last about two weeks in a cool room.

Forcing in water: Always leave at least the thickness of one finger between the base of the bulb and the liquid. The humidity of this air layer is sufficient for proper development of the roots. The aerating layer also prevents rotting.

Flowers at Christmas? Garden centers sell specially prepared prechilled bulbs that shorten the forcing time, allowing you to enjoy hyacinths as early as December. But be sure to plant these treated bulbs as soon as you buy them. If they are exposed to warm conditions for too long, they won't produce the extra-early blooms you want.

If your hyacinths are flowering on short stems, force them to grow long-necked ones. Before the hyacinths bloom, place the cardboard rolls from paper towels or toilet paper over their stems to force them to elongate toward the light. When they reach the height you want, remove the roll; they will then bloom on their long stems.

Don't throw away your forced hyacinths after they've flowered indoors. Keep them well lit and well watered and feed with liquid fertilizer. After the foliage has yellowed and died back, plant the bulbs outdoors to bloom the following season. You may have only a few flowers the first year, but the spikes will become more robust with each succeeding year—and eventually bloom as beautifully as they did the first time.

When you plant hyacinths outdoors, the smaller the bulbs, the better. Small bulbs are less expensive than the larger, premium-quality ones. And although their flower spikes may be less showy, they grow even and full. They are also less likely than their top-heavy relatives to sustain damage from wind and rain.

Repair bulbs that have been damaged from digging. If the wound is superficial, dust with wood ashes or sand, and let it dry. If the wound is deep—or even if the bulb is cut in half—store the fragments, cut sides up, in a cool, dry place. Small bulbs will develop on the surface of each piece. Plant them in the fall; they will grow large enough to flower in three to four years.

Planting delays? Place bulbs in the vegetable compartment of your refrigerator, where they will keep for two weeks. Wrap them in paper towels so that their pungent skins won't impart their smell to the food.

HYDRANGEAS

Most commonly grown are the two types of big-leaved hydrangea (*Hydrangea macrophylla*): the hortensias (or mopheads), with domed flower clusters, and the lacecaps, with flat disks of tiny florets surrounded by petals. Both flower in midsummer on the previous year's shoots. Another popular variety is *H. paniculata* 'Grandiflora', which produces showy cone-shaped panicles up to 12 inches long. Unlike big-leaved types, it flowers on the current season's shoots.

Plant hydrangeas in rich, moist soil with sun to partial shade and no competition from tree roots; water well during dry spells and keep mulched. Because some types bud early in spring, make sure that they are in a spot protected from frost. Hydrangeas look spectacular when massed, so select a place that will accommodate several plants.

The color of hydrangeas reveals the chemistry of your soil. Blue flowers indicate an acid soil (below pH 7.0), while pink indicates alkalinity (above pH 7.0). White varieties stay white, regardless of soil type. Alter the hues of your hydrangea blooms by altering the soil. For blue flowers, acidify your soil with aluminum sulfate, iron sulfate, sulfur, or a store-bought bluing solution. For pink flowers, add lime or a phosphorus-rich fertilizer to the soil to raise alkalinity. And be patient: The treatments don't work overnight; they usually take several months before having the desired effect.

To obtain brighter colors, water the roots of each of your hydrangeas with a dilute solution of 1 ounce blood meal per 1 quart water. Repeat the treatment a month after the first watering.

The dried flower heads are not only beautiful, adding interest to the winter garden, but also useful: They help protect the tender emerging buds from frost damage. Leave them on till early spring, then prune them back to just above a bud. Use spent heads for mulch or in the compost.

Prune the panicle hydrangea (*H. paniculata* 'Grandiflora') in late winter or early spring, cutting the previous year's growth to right above the new buds. Big-leaf and other hydrangeas should be rejuvenated when the plant is dormant by pruning out three to five of the oldest stems at their base. For all types, also remove any dead, damaged, or spindly wood.

IMPATIENS

Impatiens have earned their enormous popularity not only for their long-lasting displays of showy blooms but also for their ability to thrive with little sun. Plant beneath a shade tree or in borders or containers that receive partial to moderate shade. Impatiens require little special care other than rich, well-drained soil and plenty of water. Quench their hot-weather thirst often with deep waterings.

To propagate tropical or hybrid impatiens, cut a stem just below, not between, a node; cuttings taken between nodes can rot. Then remove the lower leaves and root the stem in water; place in bright, indirect light, not direct sun. Transplant carefully: The roots will be fragile.

Hybrid impatiens grow fast. Sow seeds in March instead of January or February to produce plants that are ready to set out in June—in the warm (65°F), shady conditions they require. To ensure success, don't cover the seeds in the seed tray: They need plenty of light to sprout.

A tender perennial, impatiens will bloom year-round in frost-free areas. In a greenhouse the flowers will bloom continuously as long as they are exposed to some light and steady humidity. Pinch their tips to encourage bushy growth.

For compact but well-branched plants that disappear under their flowers, pinch out the growing tips of your impatiens— even the squat varieties—before you plant them. To avoid having too few flowers at first, nip one out of every two plants, then the other two weeks later. Use the tips for cuttings to propagate new plants; they can be rooted quickly and used to fill out your groupings in a few weeks.

Delight your children by letting them grow touch-me-nots (*Impatiens biflora* and *I. pallida*) in their own corner of the garden. These Himalayan natives, also known as jewelweed, are hardy only in warm climates but self-seed freely. They produce an abundance of plump capsules that explode at the slightest touch, sending seeds on their merry way. With a single sowing you will always have plants, especially since they can adapt to any soil and exposure.

If you live in the Northeast, look in the woods for another touch-me-not (*Impatiens capensis*), which has naturalized in damp places. Bearing lovely, large flowers spotted orange and yellow, this wild impatiens can thrive until frost in any cool soil. Collect its seeds and sow them in the fall.

INVASIVE PLANTS

What makes a plant a pest? Invasive plants travel rapidly by either underground rhizomes, aboveground stolons, or seed dispersal, and crowd out less-vigorous specimens. To become

Reader's Digest Quintessential Guide

invasive, a plant must find conditions favorable for growth in its adoptive home. And limiting factors, such as insect pests or other aggressive plants, must be weak or nonexistent. Aggressive invaders inhabit every corner of the country. Among the most notorious plants are the kudzu vine, Japanese knotweed, giant reed, and water hyacinths.

Curb rampant roots by sinking metal or plastic edging a foot deep around them in the soil. Or put the plant in a 2-gallon pot before setting it in the ground. If an invader is creeping under a fence, dig an 8-inch-deep trench along its base and fasten a plastic sheet to it; bury the rest of the sheet in the trench.

To remove an unwanted vine that has crawled up a tree, first cut it off at the roots. Leave the stems and foliage to wilt for a few days, then pull them out of the tree. A rake is a handy tool for snaring the wayward strands.

Head off prolific self-sowers by deadheading the plants just after flowering. Also dig up any young volunteers as soon as they sprout. Among the plants that invade via seed are goldenrod, lamb's ears, yarrow, asters, anchusa, and columbine.

Beware of the trumpet creeper, which is wildly invasive. It finds its way under paving stones, over fences, and across lawns to pop up far from the original rooting site. Sometimes the only way to eradicate the trumpet creeper and other stubborn invaders is to cut back emerging shoots and apply a recommended herbicide to the cuts. When the stems have stopped growing, dig up and discard them.

IRISES

Irises grow from bulbs or, more commonly, from rhizomes. The rhizomatous types include bearded irises—so called for the hairs on the down-turned petals—and beardless ones, with no hairs. Among the most popular in the beardless group are the hardy, heavy-flowering Siberian iris and the water irises. The iris lacks a gene for red pigmentation but otherwise comes in many shades: from pale cream and yellow to deep blue, purple, maroon, and orange. The contrasting bands, veins, and speckles on the flowers enhance their beauty.

Irises are most striking when massed; their blooms will look like a swarm of butterflies hovering over the garden. But it's best to group only one type—bearded, beardless, or bulbous, for example—together.

Bearded irises

All they need is sun and well-drained soil. Side-dress lightly with a low-nitrogen fertilizer in early spring and late summer.

Plant or divide irises as soon as possible after blooming—sometime between July and September. This gives the plants time to take root before winter. If you plant too late, you'll get fewer blooms.

Prevent rotting stems. Plant the rhizome on a mound of soil amended with coarse sand to promote drainage. Spread the roots over the mound, fill the hole, and water.

If frost heaves the rhizomes out of the ground in winter, don't push them back down. Instead, pile a small mound of well-drained soil or coarse sand around them—but be careful not to bury them.

In cool climates, guarantee regrowth by making sure that the top part of the rhizome remains exposed to the sun. In late summer, also cut leaves back to about half their length in a fan shape.

Divide rhizomes before they become overcrowded and flowering lessens. Irises in cool-climate gardens may need to be divided only every three years, while those in warm climates may require yearly division. Check for soft, foul-smelling, or rotting rhizomes—a sign of borer damage. Make clean cuts with a sharp knife, dipping it in alcohol between cuts to avoid spreading disease. Keep only the healthy outer parts of the clump, with new growth. Let the cut rhizomes dry in the sun for several hours, then replant them 12 to 15 inches apart.

Be fastidious. Strict sanitary methods are necessary for the best bearded iris displays. Combat leaf spot, rust, or pests with fungicides or insecticides. Remove any yellowing or dying leaves promptly. Pull off dry or damaged leaves carefully, holding them as horizontally as possible. Keep iris beds free of weeds, cleaning them thoroughly both before and after planting. But take care around the rhizomes—if you nick them with a hoe or cultivator, you'll provide a doorway for diseases.

Control thrips and aphids, which can spread virus disease and reduce vigor. At the first sign of iris root borers, remove the surrounding soil and any mulching materials and dispose of them.

Siberian irises

Erosion control: With their tough, fibrous roots, Siberian irises will bind soil even on slopes. To plant, dig a deep hole and put manure on the bottom, below the root run.

Divide crowded clumps by first trimming back the foliage, then lifting with a fork. Break into sections with several shoots on each and replant. Don't let clumps get too large or you'll need an axe to divide them.

For bouquets, cut when the flowers are still buds. The blooms from this heavy-producing iris last only a few days in the vase.

Water irises

Irises that grow in water or boggy soil include the Japanese iris (*Iris ensata*), yellow flag (*I. pseudacorus*), and several native species, such as Virginia iris (*I. virginica*) and blue flag (*I. versicolor*).

While some irises grow in water up to a foot deep, most prefer the shallow margins. Prepare a planting hole with coarse peat, leaf mold, or rotted manure, and plant 2 inches deep in full sun or light shade. Mulch to suppress weeds and retain moisture. In cold climates, mulch also helps protect roots, but you will have to lift out tender types, like Louisiana hybrids, if the water freezes.

Bulbous irises

Cold-climate gardeners should lift the bulbs of bulbous Dutch and Spanish irises out of the ground after the foliage has yellowed and store them to replant in the early spring. In warmer regions these bulbs can remain in the ground all year.

If the foliage yellows during the growing season, the clumps may have become overcrowded. Lift them and divide by carefully pulling the bulbs apart, doing as little damage to the roots as possible. Replant the clumps, using wider spacing.

Watch out for black spot, which causes clumps to die off quickly. To stem the disease, plant irises in the fall in fertile, well-drained soil; avoid fertilizer. Check regularly for the symptoms: blackened bulbs and spots on the leaves. Remove infected plants and the contaminated soil.

IVY

The ideal ground cover for quickly enhancing an unattractive or little-used area, ivy grows well in even poor garden soil that is inhospitable to less vigorous plants.

Let ivy blanket a north- or west-facing wall for protection against rain and sudden shifts in temperature. Contrary to lore, it won't destroy the wall. But be careful: If the surface is already in poor shape, with cracks or bare patches, ivy will find its way in. Restore the surface of the wall as necessary.

Limit self-seeding by pruning ivy at the right time: after flowering but just before the fruit ripens to a blue-black color (generally in December). At this time it will be too late for the plant to produce more flowers and too early for the fruit that falls to the ground to sprout and spread.

Instant topiary: Cover a shape of your choice with ivy. The form can be created with a rough wood frame and covered with chicken wire. Prune only once a year, preferably in the spring, to preserve a well-defined shape.

Make a green carpet. For a quick covering, which takes one to two years, space plants 18 inches to 2 feet apart; if there's no hurry, 3-foot spacing is fine.

Don't allow ivy to invade your trees. It may be pretty—especially in its variegated forms—but it can often get the upper hand on its host, covering and smothering a tree's branches and blocking out sunlight. At most, let it climb up to the first fork in the trunk, where it can form a decorative "stocking."

Keep ivy in check by simply cutting it back with shears about 6 inches from any potential climbing surface; check new growth several times throughout the season and snip back as needed.

To root cuttings, don't take the long stems with aerial roots. Instead, use stems that have flowered but have no aerial roots or excess branching. Cut them in summer and root in pots filled with moist sand. Place them in a shaded cold frame—and plant out one year later.

JAPANESE BEETLES

These pests aren't picky. Japanese beetles eat almost every part of almost any plant. They especially love raspberries, beans, and corn, but they're also fond of apple trees, grapevines, and roses.

Check corn daily once the silk appears because the beetles feast on the tender silk. Without the silk, no pollination can occur, and no ears of corn will develop.

Plant garlic among your roses, fruit trees, and berry bushes to deter the beetles.

Cultivate soil deeply in spring and fall to kill grubs and to expose them to birds.

Handpicking can be effective in controlling adult beetles. Handpick in the cool of early morning, when they are sluggish and dew on their wings makes it harder for them to fly away. Crush them between your fingers or drop your catch in a small can of kerosene.

Invite birds into the garden by minimizing use of any broad-spectrum pesticides and by installing a birdbath, small pond, or fountain. Robins, starlings, and flickers, with the long pointed beaks needed for poking into soil, help control Japanese beetles by eating the larvae. Other birds, including cardinals and catbirds, eat the adult beetles. Make sure that fresh water is always available, but empty your bird feeders; you'll keep the birds hungry enough to snack on the beetles and grubs.

An effective botanical control for Japanese beetles is neem oil, which comes from the neem tree of India. Applied to the soil, this substance kills grubs; applied to plants, it keeps adult beetles from feeding. Use it on ornamental and edible plants.

Two more natural controls: Milky-spore disease (*Bacillus popilliae*) is a beneficial bacteria that destroys beetles while they are still at the grub stage in the soil. You can also use nematodes (*Heterorhabditis* spp.), which are microscopic parasites, to combat grub infestation. Spread them on the lawn, and they will begin infecting and killing grubs within a few days. Both controls are generally available from garden centers and mail-order sources.

Four-o'clocks, jimson weed (*Datura stramonium*), dwarf and red buckeyes, and delphiniums all attract and poison Japanese beetles. But be cautious: Both four-o'clocks and jimson weed are toxic to humans and pets as well.

Pheromone traps usually give mixed results. These scented lures sometimes attract more beetles to your garden than would normally arrive. If you try them, set the traps at least 50 feet away from any of the beetles' favorite crops.

Beetle larvae are known to dislike alkaline soil. Spread wood ashes or lime on the lawn and garden beds in the fall to raise the pH level—but first make sure that your plants won't suffer from the adjustment to soil acidity.

JERUSALEM ARTICHOKES

Not artichokes at all, Jerusalem artichokes—also called sunchokes—are actually perennial members of the sunflower family and are an American native. They are grown for their tubers—a tasty and low-calorie substitute for potatoes.

Tubers left in the ground will readily start another crop and quickly become a nuisance—especially if you've sown another vegetable nearby. It's wise to give them a permanent location where they can be contained. A good solution is to dig a 12- to 15-inch trench around the bed and install a barrier of heavy polypropylene plastic or rubber belting to stop the spread.

Dig as many as possible from the bed each year. Otherwise, tuber size and quality will soon suffer from overcrowding.

Keep their height in mind. In rich soil and partial shade, these plants can reach 6 to 12 feet tall. Pick a spot where their shade won't affect other plants. With their yellow fall flowers, they make a good screen for compost heaps or a cover for chain-link fences.

Don't store the tubers. Since their thin skins allow the roots to shrivel quickly, it's best to dig up tubers only as you need them. They can be harvested in fall until the ground freezes, then again in spring as soon as the soil has thawed. In a heavily mulched bed, the tubers can even be dug from underneath a blanket of winter snow.

Problems to watch for: The tubers are often attacked by cutworms. And root-rot fungi may occur when the soil is too wet.

KIWI

Both the common (*Actinidia deliciosa*) and hardy kiwi (*A. arguta*) are fast-growing vines that need the support of a sturdy trellis or arbor. The common kiwi, which has sweet, succulent flesh, was originally called the Chinese gooseberry. Although it is native to China, it was first grown commercially in New Zealand. There, the Chinese gooseberry was renamed after New Zealand's flightless national bird, whose feathers are quite fuzzy—just like the fruit!

The common kiwi produces the fuzzy fruits now available in many supermarkets; hardy kiwis yield sweet, green grapelike berries that have a smooth skin. To ensure fruiting, use plants of both sexes; in general, you'll need one male for up to seven females.

Kiwis need little extra attention besides pruning and regular feeding. Cut stems that fruited the previous year to 1 ½ feet in winter; control the shape with a light trimming in summer.

LADYBUGS

A gift to gardeners, ladybugs—also called lady beetles or ladybirds—dine heartily on pests in flower beds and vegetable gardens without damaging the plants. But don't expect them to be a cure-all: Their appetites are limited primarily to aphids, mealybugs, spider mites, scale, thrips, and whiteflies.

Attract ladybugs to your flower beds with marigolds, angelica, butterfly weed, yarrow, roses, and goldenrod. In the vegetable garden, good lures include cucumbers, peppers, eggplants, and tomatoes.

Buying ladybugs: Start with about 100 ladybugs per 1,000 square feet; if they have enough food and water, they'll stay and lay eggs in a few weeks. Make sure you purchase healthy specimens: Ladybugs can be infected with parasitoids, which kill their hosts and can spread rapidly through your ladybug population.

Release them in your garden in the evening, when it's calm and they have dew to drink; if it's dry, sprinkle your plants first. Place a handful around the base of a plant where you see pests. Repeat every 20 feet. If purchased ladybugs arrive before there is insect food in the garden, you can store them for three weeks in the refrigerator.

Keep ladybugs at home by offering a hibernation site. Pile dead leaves, hay, straw, or another organic mulch at the base of a fence or around plants to serve as winter lodgings.

LAVENDER

With its mounding, slightly sprawling habit, lavender is an excellent choice for softening hard structural lines. Plant it at the corners of buildings or steps, at the front or edges of raised beds, or along paths and terraces.

True lavender (*Lavandula angustifolia*) is the most common and is beloved for its gray-green foliage and spiky flower heads with their characteristic blue-purple—that is, lavender—flowers. The cultivar 'Hidcote' boasts deep purple blooms, while 'Jean Davis' has pale pink ones; these and 'Munstead' are hardy to –10°F. Other favorites are French lavender (*L. dentata*), with fringed leaves, and Spanish lavender (*L. stoechus*), which has purple bracts atop the stems instead of the usual spikes; try 'Atlas' or 'Otto Quast'. For exceptional fragrance, plant the hybrid *L. × intermedia* 'Provence'.

Give lavender full sun and light, well-drained, slightly alkaline soil. Aid drainage in heavy soil by adding a layer of coarse sand or gravel to the base of the planting hole. Feed and water sparingly.

Lavender needs a good clipping to prevent legginess. In fall or early spring, remove the dead flower spikes and an inch of the top growth; shape to form a bushy silhouette. Unless the plant is overgrown, avoid cutting into old wood, which may not regenerate.

Harvest for drying either when the buds just open or when they're in full bloom. Dry in a cool, airy spot and strip the stems.

LETTUCE

Lettuce prefers temperatures around 60° to 65°F and bolts in the heat. It needs six hours of sun daily but likes a little afternoon shade to keep it cool. Rabbits and other creatures love lettuce. Fence in the rows with chicken wire or use a scent repellent to keep them away. Some gardeners swear by interplanting with marigolds.

To grow lettuce from seed, sow it ¼ inch deep in well-drained, moderately rich soil. Start heading types indoors about six weeks before you want to set them out; sow leaf lettuce outdoors two weeks before last frost.

Place indoor seed flats in the garage to sprout. The cool floor will hold them at the ideal temperature—about 65°F.

To help seeds germinate in high temperatures, sow them in a shallow trench early in the morning. Cover with soil, water in, and lay a plank over the row to protect seeds from sun. Leave the board in place until seedlings sprout, lifting it every morning to check on them.

Set out transplants two weeks before the last frost. Plant them 7 to 8 inches apart—you can measure with outspread fingers—and protect from cold with floating row covers.

To inhibit bolting, wound the roots slightly to slow leaf growth. Use a spade with a sharp blade, piercing the soil and roots at an angle.

Lettuce needs constant moisture for good growth. If too much water washes away nutrients, turning leaves yellow, add some 15–10–10 fertilizer.

Pick lettuce in the morning, when it is at its crispest. Eat the same day for best taste or store in the refrigerator for two weeks. Harvest heading lettuces by cutting plants at the base. With leaf lettuces you can pick the outer leaves when they are still young, which encourages inner ones to grow. You can also cut a young plant an inch above the ground—it will grow back in a few weeks.

To ensure a constant supply of fresh lettuce, stagger your planting dates. Make successive plantings every three weeks until the weather turns warm.

LILIES

Lilies are reliable summer performers, bringing color and fragrance to the garden after other flowers have faded. Keep beds blossoming through the season by selecting a variety of types.

Purchasing

Horticulturally, there are nine classes of lilies. One includes the species; the others, the various hybrids: Asiatic, Aurelian, trumpet, and Oriental hybrids are the most available. The famous Madonna lily (*Lilium candidum*) and the Easter lily, hardy only in warm regions, are grown less today as hybrids gain favor. It's best to buy from mail-order suppliers and specialty growers who raise primarily bulbs. Lilies are sold in fall or early spring.

Buy by bloom time. Subasiatics and martagons bloom early—in June—followed by the Americans, Aurelians, and Orientals through August into September.

Buy flower form. Lily blooms can be shaped like trumpets, saucers, starbursts, or even tiny turbans, or "Turk's caps," with tightly reflexed petals. The flowers may face upward, flare horizontally, or hang inverted in tiers from candelabra-like stems.

Buy by color. Flowers range from pure white to deep burgundy, with pastels and eye-popping hot hues in between. While some blooms are solid colored, many are freckled, spotted, or flushed.

Buy by use. Lilies lend themselves to various planting schemes besides the flower bed. Select dwarf types, such as the coral lily, for a rock garden and shade-tolerant specimens, like the meadow lily, for a woodland garden. Many hybrids are suited to containers and cutting gardens, as well as to shrub borders.

Planting

Lilies like moist, loamy, slightly acidic soil. Pick a site with good air circulation, wind protection, and excellent drainage to prevent rotting of the bulb. If your soil is too heavy or light, dig very well-rotted manure, composted leaves, or other organic matter into the planting bed. Also work in some bonemeal or superphosphate.

Except for Madonna lilies, which are planted an inch deep, set bulbs three times as deep as they are tall. An inch-tall bulb, for example, should be buried with its tip 3 inches below the soil surface.

You can plant bulbs in fall or early spring. An exception is the Madonna lily, which goes in the ground in late August, before its rosette of leaves begins to grow.

Lilies range in height from 2 to 7 feet. Make sure you locate tall types in the back of the bed, where they won't block out shorter specimens and where the plants in front will hide their spent foliage. Underplant lilies with noncompeting companions, like primroses, violets, or baby's breath—these will keep lily roots cool and support thin lily stems.

Reader's Digest Quintessential Guide

Maintenance

Keep lilies moist—but not soaked—until they bloom. Water less after they flower, but don't let bulbs dry out. To protect foliage from diseases, use a soaker hose to direct moisture to the roots, not the leaves.

Feed in spring, just as the "nose"—the asparagus-like shoot—appears. Gently scratch in a scant tablespoon of low-nitrogen fertilizer (5–10–10) around each plant, taking care not to injure the nose or shallow stem roots; water it in. Give the plants a light supplementary feeding just at bloom time.

If you want to stake lilies, do so in spring, inserting a green metal or bamboo stake carefully by each stem so as not to injure the bulb. The stake should reach about 9 inches below the flowers. Tie in loosely with a figure-eight loop.

Warm head, cool feet. While lilies need sun to bloom, their roots must be kept cool and moist. Mulch with shredded bark, pine needles, leaf mold, or composted manure.

Lilies are beset by only two serious diseases: lily virus, which is spread by aphids, and botrytis, a fungus that disfigures and kills foliage. To control aphids, water a systemic insecticide into the soil or spray plants with rotenone. To prevent botrytis, provide good air circulation around plants and spray with a fungicide every two weeks. Note that lilies are most susceptible to botrytis as they begin their early spring growth and their foliage is soft.

When cutting blooms for arrangements, leave at least one-third of the stem on the plant so that the foliage can replenish the bulb. Place right away in a vase of water; blooms will last a week or more.

Remove flower heads after blooming unless you want to collect seed. Cut the stem right beneath the blooms, leaving the stalk. Cut off stalks after the foliage has withered completely. Doing so will help keep diseases at bay.

In cold climates, prevent frost heaves with a deep layer of straw, conifer needles, or chopped leaves. If shoots emerge

Propagate lilies by scaling

1. Select a bulb with healthy, uninjured outer scales and detach them.

2. Dust with fungicide and place in a plastic bag filled with damp peat or vermiculite; punch holes for ventilation. Store at 60° to 70°F for six to twelve weeks. Once small bulblets have formed at the base of the scales and the roots are ½ inch long, place the bag in the refrigerator for two to three months.

3. In spring, plant the scales with the bulblets attached in beds or pots. They will grow into bulbs big enough to bloom in one to two years.

prematurely in early spring, cover them with a cloche, basket, or other device. Work around the shoots gently—if you snap them off, you'll have no blooms.

Propagation

Propagate by scaling. See "Propagate lilies by scaling" above.

Increase with bulblets: Most lilies form bulblets along the underground stem. Gently detach them and plant in beds or pots to increase your stock.

A special case: the tiger lily (*L. lancifolium*) and some of its hybrids form beadlike bulbils in the leaf axils as well as bulblets underground. Harvest bulbils as flowers fade and plant in beds or pots.

Divide lilies only if they are overcrowded. Carefully lift the dormant clumps and separate the bulbs, planting each individually.

LIME

Lime is most often used to add calcium to the soil. It raises soil pH, allowing gardeners with acidic soil to grow plants that need neutral or alkaline conditions. Lime also helps open up thick clay soil to water and air penetration, and speeds decomposition of organic matter. Some gardeners lime their lawns and garden beds annually, which is wasteful and can encourage weed growth. Have your soil tested; if the pH reading falls below 6.0, add 5 pounds of ordinary or dolomitic lime per 100 square feet. If a soil test indicates a shortage of calcium and magnesium, apply dolomitic lime. Both nutrients are often deficient in sandy, acidic soils.

How to apply: Lime won't move upward in soil, so don't dig it in deeply. Apply by hand or spreader, then water in; use it in any season. Ordinary and dolomitic lime take two to three months to work, but the benefits last a few years. If you need to raise the pH drastically, make several applications over time, using no more than 5 pounds per 100 square feet at once.

Don't apply lime and manure to the same soil in the same year. Lime interacts with the nitrogen in manure to release ammonia, which can damage plants.

Lime is caustic in all forms. Wear a dust mask and protective clothes when handling it, and wash it immediately off your skin.

Dust plants with hydrated lime to fight pests and fungus. Apply with a coffee-can duster: punch small holes in the base, fill with lime, and cover the top with the plastic lid. To help it stick, shake lime over plants when their leaves are wet with dew.

MANURE

Manure is invaluable as a soil builder and fertilizer, containing the three primary nutrients—nitrogen, phosphorus, and potassium. Ask at local farms, stables, or feedlots. Make sure your source hasn't treated the manure with pesticides or the animals with medicines, though. Never use manure from pets. Alternatively, buy processed manure in bags at garden shops. Some raw manure, like that of poultry, is so nitrogen-rich that it can burn plants; it may also harbor weed seeds. Let it age at least six months for "rotted" and a year for "well-rotted." Put fresh manure in a pile and water it. Cover with a tarp to prevent nutrients from leaching out when it rains. Turn the pile occasionally to speed decomposition.

As manure decays, it releases heat, which kills weed seeds. Measure the temperature at the center of the pile with a soil thermometer. If the reading is below 150°F, add water and a nitrogen source, such as soybean meal, and turn thoroughly into the pile. Bird and bat guano are the "hottest" manures, with the highest nitrogen content. Rabbit, poultry, and sheep manures are a bit less hot, while those from cows, pigs, and horses are relatively "cold." Add wood chips, sawdust, dead leaves, or another high-carbon material to aging manure, especially in summer. It will help alleviate the unpleasant smell.

A three-year rotation: Enrich a third of your vegetable garden with rotted manure. In the first year, use the space for heavy feeders, like eggplant, cabbage, peppers, spinach, and squash. The next year, plant it with carrots, tomatoes, green beans, and other vegetables that need slightly less fertile soil. The third year, grow light feeders such as garlic, turnips, onions, and radishes.

Manure tea is a rich liquid fertilizer that gives plants a quick boost. Put a shovelful of raw manure in a permeable bag made of burlap or pantyhose, tie the top, and steep in a barrel or garbage can of water for a week. If you use it every time

Reader's Digest Quintessential Guide

you water, dilute it by half. Use full strength to feed plants periodically, taking care not to let it splash on foliage.

MARIGOLDS

Marigolds are one of the most carefree annuals, performing well from seed or transplants in a warm, sunny spot and any well-drained soil. The compact signet marigold and the mid-size French types are suited to bed edgings and containers. The taller African marigolds are best for the back of the border or for a cutting garden. When planting different solid-color marigolds, mix in a few with bicolored blooms to tie the scheme together.

Start seed indoors no more than four weeks before you want to set plants out. Otherwise the seedlings may become leggy. Sow seed directly outdoors once the soil has warmed to near 70°F. Sow in shallow trenches and cover with ½ inch of soil. Keep moist; seedlings should sprout in about two weeks. Water marigolds often until they are well established, then water only weekly if rainfall is inadequate.

Start pinching out blooms when they first appear to promote budding and a bushy shape. Deadhead and keep pinching until frost to keep marigolds flowering heavily.

With their large pom-pom blooms, African varieties can tip over from their own weight. Instead of staking each plant, try deep planting. Strip the leaves from the bottom 3 to 4 inches of the stem, dig a deep hole, and set in the plant with the stripped portion below the soil line.

MELONS

The seeds of all melons—watermelons, cantaloupes, and honeydews—sprout best when planted with their pointy tips facing down. For a head start, sow seed indoors four to six weeks before last frost. Bury three seeds ½ inch deep in 3-inch pots filled with compost and sandy soil; keep moist and warm, at about 70°F. Thin to one sprout per pot and plant out two weeks after last frost.

Sow outdoors when the soil temperature reaches 70°F. Sow in hills, using five seeds per hill and thinning to two or three. Leave 3 feet between hills; allow 6 feet between rows for watermelon and 3 feet for all other types. Soil should be loose, loamy, and well drained; add a few shovelfuls of rotted manure or compost per hill.

Plant melons in the sunniest spot and cover with a floating row cover, which both protects against cold snaps and thwarts pests. Remove the covers once plants flower so that pollinating insects can do their work and you'll have a crop.

Keep melons off the soil to prevent rot. Slip a board or flat tile underneath the fruits once they reach the size of an orange. Heat-absorbing tiles will also provide extra warmth in cool climates.

Mulch; don't weed. Because working around vines may disturb the transmission of nutrients to the fruits, stop weeding once the vines begin to sprawl. Just spread a heavy layer of straw around plants; it will adequately suppress weeds.

For the best fruits, allow only four or five melons to ripen on each plant. Cut off all the other young fruits. Give melons an inch of water weekly until three weeks before harvest; then withhold moisture to help concentrate the sugars.

Is it ripe? Press against the blossom end (not the end with the stem). It will give slightly and smell sweet when the fruit is ripe. Or you can knock against a watermelon with your knuckles; a ripe one will sound hollow.

MINT

Plant mint in rich, moist, cool soil in partial shade. In addition to peppermint and spearmint, add lesser-known types for variety and extra fragrance. Apple mint has downy foliage;

orange mint emits a citrusy aroma; and the white-rimmed leaves of pineapple mint smell fruity-sweet.

Plant mint near entrances to your house—it will prevent ants from coming in. Drive aphids and caterpillars from the garden with a homemade pesticide. In a blender, mix 8 ounces of mint leaves with 1 quart water. Strain and spray on plants; repeat every ten days.

A rambunctious grower, mint can quickly become invasive. To contain the roots, plant mint in a large pot and bury it, setting the rim slightly below the soil line. Or sink plastic edging strips a foot deep around the roots.

Clip off young shoots regularly to promote bushiness. Prune established plants especially hard to stimulate growth of tender leaves. Harvest mint until a few weeks before the first frost of fall.

MISTLETOE

Christmas wouldn't be complete without this native plant, a traditional green used in kissing balls and other decorations. But mistletoe (*Phoradendron* spp.) is an invasive parasite that sucks the sap from its host tree, causing weakness or death. To get rid of it, pull or cut it out, removing all roots. Do it early— the smaller the plant, the easier the removal.

Be cautious. Mistletoe stems, leaves, and berries are all poisonous, and should be considered dangerous. If you use the plant in holiday decorations, keep it away from children by hanging it from a doorway or ceiling.

To grow mistletoe, start by selecting a host tree that is at least twenty years old. Collect ripe white berries from mistletoe that is already growing on another tree of the same variety as your host. Find a branch on the host that is 5 feet off the ground and about 6 inches in diameter; smash the berries against the branch's underside. The sticky pulp will harden and help seeds adhere to the bark. After seeds have germinated, they will sprout and eventually invade the host.

MULCH

Why mulch? It insulates the soil from temperature extremes, keeping it warmer in winter and cooler in summer. Mulch also minimizes erosion, moisture loss, and weed growth. Perhaps its most important role is preventing frost damage. Not only will mulched plants not be heaved out of the ground by alternate freezing and thawing but also they won't be tempted to emerge prematurely during a brief winter warm-up.

When to mulch: For perennials, trees, and shrubs, you can leave mulch in place year-round. For vegetables and annuals, wait until the soil warms. For vegetables and bulbs overwintering in the ground, wait till the soil freezes, then remove it in spring.

Usually 2 to 3 inches are enough. If erosion or weeds are a persistent problem or if you're overwintering tender specimens, spread 4 to 6 inches. In permanent installations, just refresh the top each year to maintain the proper depth.

What to use: Many gardeners prefer ornamental mulches for year-round use or for flower beds. Shredded bark, wood chips, and cocoa or walnut shells are attractive but expensive. For seasonal use in the vegetable patch, hay, straw, chopped leaves, ground corncobs, and even shredded newpaper are inexpensive and effective—and you can turn them into the soil at summer's end. (Newsprint is effective as long as it doesn't contain colored ink. Chop it first with a lawn mower or shredder.)

What not to use: Never use a mulch that mats down or cakes together—it will prevent water, air, and nutrients from penetrating the soil. Materials like coffee grounds, peat moss, grass clippings, or sawdust should be mixed with a less-dense mulch before being used.

Match your mulch to the plants. Acid-lovers, including rhododendron and camellias, appreciate an acidic mulch. Try pine needles, oak-leaf mold, shredded oak leaves, or composted sawdust from cypress or oak. On plants that don't need acid, use neutral materials like buckwheat hulls, corncobs, or straw; if you're using an acidic mulch, add a little lime.

Dead leaves can be used in several ways. Spread small leaves right on the beds. Let large leaves age a year or so to make nutritious leaf-mold mulch. Or chop large leaves to make them easier to handle. If you don't have a shredder, run a lawn mower over a pile of leaves or pack them in a garbage can and chop with a string trimmer.

Arborists and utility companies that trim trees around power lines often have surplus wood chips ground from felled trees. Also ask your municipality—some have leaf-composting or brush-chipping sites and offer free mulch to the community.

Aluminized plastic mulch helps repel pests—insects passing by are confused by the light and fly away. Make your own mulch by placing sheets of aluminum foil around plants and anchoring them with stones.

The latest trend is geotextiles—permeable woven or bonded fabrics that blanket the soil and perform all the functions of organic mulches. They are particularly effective in suppressing weeds and are safe to use around permanent plantings like shrubs. Because they degrade if exposed to light and are unattractive, top them with shredded bark or wood chips.

Black plastic mulch is best for vegetable gardens. Its radiant heat warms the soil—up to 3°F higher than unmulched soil—and keeps dirt from splashing on plants, which can cause rot. Lay it on the bed and make slits for transplants or seeds; fold it up at season's end and reuse the following year. But take note: Since rain can't pass through, you'll need to water beneath the plastic with a soaker hose or drip line.

Before mulching roses, soak mulch in a dilute solution of an ounce of bleach per gallon of water for one hour. This will help discourage black spot.

Be aware that some mulches, such as wood chips and sawdust, deplete nitrogen from the soil when they begin decaying. Dig in ammonium nitrate, blood meal, rotted manure, or another nitrogen source before spreading these mulches. And mulching doesn't mean you can neglect the garden. You will still need to weed, water, fertilize, and monitor pests and diseases.

Don't pile mulch too close to trunks or stems. It can smother plants, promote rot, and let slugs, mice, and other pests hide near a food source. And don't use plastic mulch around shrubs and other hardy plants. Because it is not permeable, it cuts off air and water to roots; it also causes soil to heat up excessively in summer.

NARCISSUS

Although "daffodil" is often applied to all members of the genus *Narcissus*, it is just one of the many plant groups in this diverse bulb family. There are about twenty-five species and thousands of varieties blooming between February and May. All narcissus have a central trumpet, or corona, but its size, color, and shape varies from plant to plant. Narcissus are one of the few plants that most deer don't like. Plant several species: not every one is deer proof. Rodents also hate them. Interplant narcissus with tulips, hyacinth, and other bulbs beloved by chipmunks, mice, and moles. Because narcissus are slightly toxic and unpalatable, pests will generally leave them—and neighboring plants—alone.

Grow narcissus as you would any spring bulb. Plant in fall at twice the bulb depth in rich, well-drained soil. Note that they can tolerate more shade than other bulbs. The best way to plant narcissus is in naturalistic drifts, with dozens of bulbs creating meadows of color. But keep in mind that narcissus foliage must be allowed to die back naturally. So locate bulbs where fading foliage won't interfere with lawn mowing or be a distraction. You can also overplant with a ground cover, ferns, or perennials. If a spring cold snap threatens to injure plants, protect them with a mound of dry peat moss.

Divide narcissus every four years in early summer, after the foliage has died back. Lift the clump with a fork, shake off soil, and let bulbs dry in the shade for a few days. Pull off the bulblets and replant.

NASTURTIUMS

Train a vining variety of nasturtium (*Tropaeolum* spp.) to adorn a blank wall—the 10-foot-long runners will cover a trellis with lily-pad-like leaves and funnel-shaped flowers. Set the tender plants out after all danger of frost has passed in well-drained soil amended with compost. Select a sunny location but provide afternoon shade in very hot climates; water well till established. They will bloom until frost.

To make a pretty pyramid, drive a stake into the center of a wooden barrel. Stretch about a dozen pieces of string from the stake to the edges of the container and fasten with tacks. Plant climbing nasturtiums around the barrel perimeter and train the vines up the strings. Use as a centerpiece in an herb garden or on a patio.

Mix with vegetables. Plant bush nasturtiums between rows of vegetables, spacing them at about 12 to 18 inches. They make a pretty ground cover and are said to repel some insects—and their blooms are edible!

While transplants are readily available, nasturtiums are so easy to grow from seed that you can sow them directly in the garden. Sow once soil warms in ½ inch of average, well-drained soil. Thin seedlings to 6 inches; protect from frost.

NATIVE PLANTS

The word "native" refers to plants that grow in the same habitat in which they originated; "exotic" plants, conversely, are those growing in a different area from where they originated. Plants can be native to a continent, state, or region. Just because a plant is native to your area doesn't mean it's suited to your site. Always consider the plant's growing requirements before including it in your garden.

Never collect plants from the wild. More than 2,000 native American plants are endangered or protected—digging them up may be against the law. And many, like the lady's slipper, are difficult to transplant from their natural habitats. Check with a wildflower conservation society about endangered species in your area.

You may collect seed from the wild, which helps a species spread. But take only small quantities—no more than 10 percent of the seed in a given area—so that the plants can replenish their populations naturally.

When buying native plants, make sure your source is selling stock propagated from seed or by vegetative means—not plants dug in the wild.

NITROGEN

Nitrogen is one of the three primary plant nutrients. Although it is present in the air, plants must take it up through the soil—either from chemical fertilizers or from the breakdown of organic matter. Because nitrogen is rapidly depleted, it must be replenished regularly. Nitrogen (N) is the first element listed on a fertilizer label; the others are phosphorus (P) and potassium (K). The first number—as in 6–2–1—indicates the percentage of nitrogen in the total mass.

The best organic sources of nitrogen are manure, blood meal, cottonseed meal, hoof and horn meal, fish emulsion, and soybean meal. Good sources found in your own backyard are leaf mold and grass clippings. Chemical sources of nitrogen include ammonium sulfate, ammonium nitrate, calcium nitrate, and sodium nitrate.

Green manures, like white clover and rye, are raised to add nitrogen to the soil. Sow seed wherever you want to enrich the soil and let grow until plants are 6 inches tall. Cut them to the soil line, then turn under. They will decay rapidly to release nitrogen, so wait at least a week before planting.

Poultry feathers make a nitrogen-rich fertilizer. Place them in a tub; top with a plastic screen and a few stones to hold them down. Cover with water and let steep in a shady spot. After two months, strain and use the liquid to fertilize plants.

Sour the soil with ammonium sulfate. Use it on plants needing acidic conditions, like rhododendrons, azaleas, and camellias.

Add a chemical or organic nitrogen source—preferably manure—to the compost pile to speed decomposition.

Let it sit. There's no need to dig nitrogen fertilizer into the soil. Water it in or let the rain do it for you.

Get a jump on spring by applying an organic nitrogen source in late fall. It will break down slowly and be available in the soil by planting time the following year.

How much is too much? You'll know you have applied excessive nitrogen if blossoms are sparse and foliage grows too fast and lush, which makes plants more vulnerable to pests, disease, and environmental stress. There is no antidote; rain and frequent watering will eventually wash nitrogen away.

Not enough? Plants deprived of nitrogen will look stunted and spindly, with pale foliage that eventually turns yellow and dies. Correct the shortage by adding an inch of rotted manure to the soil and by spraying foliage with fish emulsion weekly until symptoms disappear.

OKRA

A tropical shrub that can reach a full 6 feet tall, okra is an edible cousin of hibiscus and cotton. It's grown as an annual vegetable for its tasty seedpods, which are preceded by showy, funnel-form yellow blooms up to 3 inches wide. Nearly all varieties are early producers: they begin bearing about sixty days after sowing and continue until frost.

Okra thrives in heat and sun. The seeds require warm soil (70°F) to germinate, and the plants won't set seed unless the air temperature is at least 75°F. Although it is a fixture in vegetable patches in the Deep South, okra will succeed in any region where corn will grow.

To encourage germination, soak seeds overnight in tepid water or nick them lightly with a file. Sow seeds ½ inch deep in sandy soil and an inch in heavy soil at 3 inches apart; thin to 18 inches. Okra isn't fussy about soil, but it will respond well to fertile garden loam.

Southern gardeners can double their harvest by starting their first crop in early spring and their second in June. An alternative to resowing is to cut back the first crop almost to ground level; if watered and fed, the plants will regrow.

Watch out for stinkbugs—also known as the harlequin bug. Pick them off by hand and destroy them.

Basic care: Feed okra heavily with a high-potassium fertilizer in spring, especially if you're growing it in light or sandy soil. Then give it supplementary feedings once a month with manure tea or a side-dressing of rotted manure. During the hottest days of summer, give plants at least an inch of water each week. Once plants reach 6 inches tall, mulch heavily to conserve moisture and keep weeds under control. Harvest often. Pick pods every few days during the peak of the season. They are at their best when young and tender—about 2 to 4 inches long for most varieties. Clip with a pruner or sharp knife and wear gloves if the plant has spines. Remove and compost any mature pods you may have missed so that the plant will keep producing. Late in the season, allow the pods at the top of the plant to mature until dry. Their interesting shape makes a novel addition to dried arrangements.

Reader's Digest Quintessential Guide

OLEANDER

A Mediterranean native, this flowering evergreen shrub is a favorite in warm climates—especially in coastal areas—because it tolerates heat, drought, wind, and salt spray. The tough, fast-growing plant requires little attention once established. Some oleander varieties grow to about 12 feet tall with an equal spread. Use the plant in hedges or as a screen, and let it form a mound.

Oleander roots easily. All you have do is put a cutting in a jar of water and wait for roots to form.

Oleander is extremely toxic. The seeds, foliage, and flowers are all poisonous, and some people get a skin reaction even from contact with the leaves. Keep children and animals away from the plants, and wear gloves and long sleeves when it's time to prune them.

Gray or brown scale insects commonly infest oleander. Remove by hand with a soft brush dipped in soapy water, then rinse. Or treat with pyrethrum.

ONIONS

In the North, plant long-day onions, which require as much as sixteen hours of sunlight per day. In the South, use short-day types, which need only twelve hours. Pick from bulb and bunching onions. The familiar bulb onion may be white, yellow, or red and range in size from tiny pearls to outsized Spanish types. Bunching onions, called scallions or green onions, are grown for their top stalks and harvested before the bulbs form fully.

Start seeds indoors in pots eight to twelve weeks before the last frost. Sow four seeds per pot; water and feed. If you sow in trays, thin when plants are 4 inches tall to 1 inch apart. Outdoors, sow seed ½ inch deep and 1 inch apart in loose, fertile soil; thin to 4 inches. Start two weeks before the last spring frost or four weeks before the first fall frost.

Set out seedlings in early spring, as soon as soil can be worked and the danger of frost is past; the soil should be at least 45°F. Space your home-grown plants, with four in a plug, 1 foot apart. Space individual purchased seedlings 2 inches deep and 4 inches apart. After four weeks, brush back a little soil to expose the tops of the bulbs; this will help them develop.

When planting sets, look for bulbs about ½ inch in diameter. Plant with the pointy tips up 1 inch deep and 4 inches apart. A pound of sets is enough for a 50-foot row.

Lots at first, a little later on. Water and feed with a high-nitrogen fertilizer—fish emulsion, for example—early in the season to develop large plants; it will encourage the growth of large bulbs. Cut back water and food at midsummer; bulbs will ripen better in the drier, less-fertile conditions.

Weed carefully, as shallow onion roots are easily damaged. Pull weeds up and away from bulbs by hand. Or use a sharp hoe to cut them off—but don't dig into the soil. You can also spread mulch, but be sure to remove it when the bulbs start ripening.

Speed ripening by loosening the soil around the bulbs with a hoe two to three weeks before the harvest. Once tops turn yellow, bend the leaves over with the back of a rake; this will divert the plant's energy to the bulbs instead of the stems. In a day or so, after tops have turned brown, lift the bulbs with a fork. If it's sunny, let them dry a little on the bed. Lay the tops of one row over the bulbs of another to keep them from burning.

To cure bulbs, drape the tops in a pail weighted with stones and let the bulbs dangle over the rim. Once the skins are dry and the tops have withered, in about a week, cut away the stems—they'll fall in the bucket for easy disposal in the compost pile. Don't forget to remove the stones. If space is limited, fit a wooden frame with a large-mesh grill. Loop the onion stems through the holes to hold them in place. Once bulbs are dry, cut or pull them off as you need them. Properly cured bulbs will last from a month to a year, depending on the variety.

ORCHIDS

Orchids are commonly perceived as delicate and demanding. But thanks to modern cultural techniques, home gardeners can grow these exotic beauties with only moderate effort. Most orchids require a warm environment (60°–80°F), high humidity, twelve to fourteen hours of light daily, protection from direct summer sun, and good air circulation.

The two types: Terrestrial orchids grow in the ground; most are hardy enough to be raised outdoors in the North. Tropical orchids are tender and primarily epiphytic—that is, their roots thrive in organic matter lodged in tree limbs or rocks and exposed to the air. Grow tropicals outdoors in warm climates; in cold areas, raise them in a greenhouse, solarium, windowsill, or window-mounted mini greenhouse.

Terrestrial orchids

For success outdoors, plant each specimen in an environment that resembles its native habitat, such as a bog, woodland, or meadow. Provide winter protection with a heavy mulch of leaves or peat moss.

Never collect terrestrial orchids from the wild; buy only from nurseries. Look for healthy, established specimens that are ready to flower. Seedlings may not adjust to your garden and can take years to bloom.

Tropical orchids

Pot tropical orchids in a special medium that allows quick drainage and air circulation; they will not survive in a typical potting soil. Orchid fiber may include fir bark, sphagnum moss, tree fern fiber, perlite, and charcoal. Use plastic pots with drainage holes; clay pots dry out too quickly. For the best blooms and growth, apply a special orchid fertilizer once every two to three weeks.

Provide good air circulation; it's essential for healthy orchids. If you can't open a window, use a small oscillating fan, directing it away from the plants.

Orchids love humidity. Set them atop a tray of damp pebbles, keeping the base of the pots out of the water. Water in the morning whenever the potting fiber looks dry—but never make it soggy. While you can water once a week most of the year, you may need to do it daily in summer. Use 60° to 70°F water. You can also mist them lightly each morning.

Repot orchids every two years, once the fiber breaks down or the plant outgrows its container. The best time to transplant is after the plant has flowered. Groom orchids when you repot them. Prune off any dead roots with clean, sterile scissors. Divide overgrown specimens so that each new orchid plant has three or more pseudo-bulbs—the swollen stems—and some new growth.

Orchid roots are a good indicator of the plant's health. They should be firm and white, with green tips. Soft brown roots may mean the orchid has received excess food or too much or too little water. It also may mean the potting medium has decayed and needs to be changed.

ORGANIC FERTILIZERS

Organic fertilizers are garden foods derived from plants, animals, and minerals. They supply nutrients slowly, leach out gradually, and won't burn plants. They are also nontoxic to earthworms. Instead of feeding plants directly, organic fertilizers feed microorganisms in the soil, which break down the organic matter and release nutrients to plants. As with chemical fertilizers, use organic ones to promote fertility—not to compensate for bad soil. Although some types, like manure, improve soil structure, no fertilizer can correct fundamental

Reader's Digest Quintessential Guide

problems with drainage or tilth. Some fertilizers, like bonemeal, are dry granules or powders; they can be spread on or dug into the soil. Others, like fish emulsion, are liquid; these are watered into the soil or sprayed directly on foliage.

Buy organic fertilizers in garden shops or catalogs. Choose from complete fertilizers containing the three basic elements (nitrogen, phosphorus, and potassium) or special foods that supply one nutrient, like nitrogen-rich blood meal. With organic fertilizers, the sum of the N–P–K, or nutrient, ratio (such as 6–2–1) should not exceed 15.

Apply fertilizers when you're preparing beds or holes for planting. With hardy trees, shrubs, and perennials, apply in early spring. For heavy feeders, you can also side-dress with light supplementary doses of fertilizer throughout the season. Apply bonemeal close to the root zone, using the finest-ground product you can find. Work it into the holes when planting trees, shrubs, roses, and bulbs.

Cottonseed meal can lower soil pH. Use it only on plants that prefer acidic soil, like rhododendrons.

Sweeten acid soil with wood ash or rock phosphate. Either of these amendments will raise pH by at least one point.

ORGANIC GARDENING

Organic gardeners like to quote an old Chinese proverb: "The best fertilizer in the garden may be the gardener's own shadow." It's their belief that the daily attendance of a living presence, as opposed to a chemical or artificial one, may be the best tonic growing plants can have. The tenet of organic gardening is using nature as a guide and disturbing the environment as little as possible. It involves using preventive techniques to avoid problems and treating any pests, diseases, or nutrient deficiencies without synthetic chemicals.

The basis of organic gardening is good soil. Have it tested and adjust the pH as needed. Use organic fertilizers and improve soil structure by incorporating compost, manure, or other organic matter. Guard against erosion with mulch.

Compost, compost, compost! It's the best way to provide organic matter to the soil and reduce the amount of garden waste flowing into landfills and dumps.

Away with weeds! Hand pick, hoe up, or smother weeds with mulch to keep them from harboring pests and diseases and robbing your plants of nutrients.

Shop smart. Buy plants, whether hybrid or open-pollinated types, that are resistant to pests and diseases and tolerant of the growing conditions in your garden.

Pest control

Keep pests off plants with barriers. Use floating row covers, fine-mesh netting, burlap, cardboard, or aluminum foil. Even a circle of tar paper under a plant will keep some insects from doing damage or laying eggs.

Hand picking is often all that's needed to reduce insect populations. Pluck pests off plants and squash them. Or you can drop them in a pail of soapy water.

Plant food sources, such as angelica and morning glory, to attract ladybugs, lacewings, and other predators that eat fellow insects. Or buy beneficials from catalogs. As long as nectar and their favorite pests are available, they'll stick around. Birds, bats, frogs, lizards, spiders are also good allies. Plant asters and goldenrod, which spiders like for their web sites; leave a patch of plant debris in a garden corner where spider eggs can overwinter.

You can brew your own pesticides in the kitchen by blending ½ cup hot peppers or garlic with 2 cups water and spraying it on infested plants. A strong stream of plain water is also effective in destroying aphids, mealybugs, and red spider mites.

Use biological controls, like *Bacillus thuringiensis* (Bt), and biological poisons, such as rotenone, to combat serious pest infestations.

Disease control

Sanitary practices help prevent the spread of fungal, bacterial, and viral diseases. Wash tools in a solution of 2 tablespoons bleach to 1 quart water or wipe surfaces with isopropyl alcohol. Also keep the garden clean: Remove infected plants and autumn debris, where diseases can lurk through winter.

Be diverse. Planting a wide range of specimens helps keep diseases from running rampant through the garden.

The way to water: Some soilborne diseases are spread when they are splashed on foliage during overhead watering. Use a soaker hose or drip irrigation and water only in the morning. Also use mulch to keep soil on the ground—not on plants.

There's no cure for bacterial and viral diseases; you must destroy the plants. You can control fungi, however, with nontoxic organic solutions made from baking soda, copper, sulfur, and lime.

PARSLEY

Parsley is a vitamin-rich biennial that comes in two forms: flat-leaf and curly-leaf. The flat-leaf type (*Petroselinum crispum* var. *neapolitanum*), also called Italian parsley, has a stronger flavor and is preferred for hot dishes. Curly-leaf parsley (*Petroselinum crispum* var. *crispum*) has a milder flavor and adds a fresh "green" taste to cold dishes.

Parsley seeds can take six weeks to sprout and need moisture to break dormancy. Speed germination by soaking the seeds in lukewarm water for several hours before sowing. To ease handling of the tiny seeds, dry them off and mix them with sand or dried coffee grounds. Sow them outdoors in ¼ inch of soil and cover the row with a board to keep seeds moist and cool. Lift the board daily to check for sprouts; they should emerge in about a week.

Sow some radish seed in the furrow with the parsley. Radishes sprout first, marking the row so that you won't disturb the parsley seed while hoeing.

Keep leaves clean. Mulch parsley plants with straw to keep soil from splashing on the leaves during rainstorms or watering. To dislodge any grit before using parsley, swish harvested stems in cool water.

PEAS

Peas prefer cool weather and stop maturing once temperatures reach 70°F. In the North, plant as soon as the soil can be worked in spring; in the South, plant in fall. Sow seed ½ inch deep and 2 inches apart in rows that are 3 feet apart. Treat pea seeds with a bacterial inoculant powder to help them fix nitrogen from the air. Doing so will increase your crop yields. Because peas will fix nitrogen in the soil, they are a good crop to plant before rotating corn or other heavy feeders in the same garden space.

Peas come in three forms: garden peas (also called shelling peas), snap peas, and snow peas—the latter two with crisp, edible pods. Select from dwarf, midsize, or tall types and early, mid-season, or late varieties—peas mature between fifty-five and seventy days.

A pea tepee. A decorative and practical way to plant peas is in a ring around a tepee. Use slender tree branches with plenty of twigs. Push 5-foot-tall stakes about 1 foot into the soil.

Other supports: Give tall, vining varieties an arbor to climb on. Support dwarf or midsize bush plants with netting, string, or a chicken-wire trellis that is 4 feet tall. Or grow them along a chain-link fence.

The pea weevil is a common pest. Dust dampened or dew-laden foliage with lime or rotenone to repel the tiny, brown beetles.

Reader's Digest Quintessential Guide

Picking: Harvest shelling and snap peas about three weeks after blossoms appear; the pods will be plump and bumpy. Pick snow peas when the pods are still flat. Snip or gently pull the pods from their stalks. The sweetest peas are those eaten immediately; the sugar turns quickly to starch.

PEAT MOSS

Derived from partly decayed sphagnum moss, peat has many garden uses. It loosens and aerates soil—making it ideal for potting mixes—and helps retain moisture. It also works well as a mulch and makes an excellent insulator.

Peat moss is sold dried and pressed in plastic-covered bales and can be hard to scoop out. Loosen with a hand cultivator before digging in with a shovel. Moisten it thoroughly before using as a soil amendment or mulch, then keep it moist.

How much moss for mulch? A 6-cubic-foot bale of peat moss will cover about 300 square feet when spread an inch deep.

Protect tender plants in a peat-moss jacket. Ring the plant with a wire cage and line with plastic. Shovel in dry peat to cover the plant. Tent the top loosely with a plastic sheet to shed water but permit airflow.

Start bulbs in the bag. Give dahlias and other summer-flowering bulbs a head start by planting them in a bag of peat outdoors. Cut open the bag, wet well, and nestle the bulbs in the peat. If a cold spell threatens, cover the opening with a board.

Because peat moss is acidic, it is ideal for heath, heather, and their other family members: rhododendrons, mountain laurel, and blueberries. Dig plenty of moist peat into the planting hole and mix more into the backfill.

PEONIES

Peonies are either herbaceous or tree types. Both kinds boast ruffly blooms of white, pink, rose, or yellow, from 5 to 12 inches across. Peonies like to stay put, so select their location carefully and prepare their beds to last for years. Pick a sunny to partially shaded spot that is protected from wind. Dig to a depth of 12 inches and amend the soil generously with compost or well-rotted manure; the soil should be slightly acidic and quick draining. Mix a few handfuls of bonemeal into each hole.

Plant peonies in autumn, when their "eyes"—little red buds on the crown—are visible. Set the eyes 1 to 2 inches below the soil line, but no deeper; otherwise the plant will never bloom.

Help prevent peonies' heavy blooms from snapping in the wind by shielding the plants with an evergreen hedge. A bonus: The flowers will sparkle all the more before the dark-green backdrop.

To keep a row of peonies looking neat and natural, support them with a string fence. Place green stakes at the ends and in the middle of the row. Run soft green twine between the stakes at two or three different heights. Be sure to set up the fence early—before the buds break.

To keep the blossoms from falling over, let peonies grow through the metal support rings available at garden centers. Or make your own: cut a circle from a piece of large-mesh grill and attach it securely to a thick bamboo stake. Position the ring close to the ground as growth begins and raise it gradually as the stems get taller.

If you must move peonies, transplant them in early fall. Lift the clump carefully with a fork and divide the roots into pieces with a knife or by hand, making sure that each has three to five eyes. Replant the divisions immediately in amended soil, with the tips of the eyes no deeper than 2 inches below soil level; water well. After the ground has frozen solid, spread a thick but airy mulch of hay, shredded oak leaves, or evergreen branches over the planting bed.

PEPPERS

These tropical natives need warmth to thrive. Start seed indoors eight weeks before you want to set out plants and keep them at about 70°F. Transplant outdoors a month after the last frost, once the soil temperature reaches at least 65°F. Don't plant peppers where you previously grew potatoes, eggplants, or tomatoes. All of these members of the nightshade family are prone to the same soilborne diseases.

Peppers like a well-aerated bed. Turn soil to 1 foot deep and amend with 20 pounds of compost per 100 feet of row.

Peppers need even, moderate moisture around their roots. Watering overhead when plants are in bloom will wash away pollen, resulting in no fruits. Water only with a drip irrigation system or soaker hose.

Spread a thick-but-light mulch, such as grass clippings or hay, to conserve moisture, but keep it a few inches from the plant base. Good mulching is especially important once the peppers bear fruit—the heavy plants tend to topple over, and mulch will keep them clean.

If you amended the soil well with compost, peppers generally don't need fertilizer. If leaves are pale, however, the plants may be suffering from a nutritional deficiency. Spray weekly with a mixture of kelp and fish emulsion until they bloom.

Pick peppers by cutting—not pulling—the ripe fruits from plants, taking about ½ inch of stem. Harvest most fruits when they are still green. While leaving a few peppers on the plant slows production, the remaining fruits will become sweeter and change color to red, yellow, or orange depending on the variety. If frost threatens, harvest any ripe peppers and cover the plants with blankets. The protection should keep the peppers producing for another week or so.

PERENNIALS

Perennials are herbaceous plants with soft, nonwoody stems that live for more than one season. The top growth dies back each winter, but the roots survive to send up new shoots in spring. Although some perennials will last only a few years, others can survive for decades. A few perennials, including santolina, lavender, and Russian sage, have semiwoody stems, but they are too insubstantial to be considered shrubs. Some perennials, such as wax begonia, zonal geraniums, alstroemeria, and calla lily are not hardy and must be grown as annuals in cold climates. But they will return year after year in hot areas.

Purchasing

While perennial plants are available from garden centers and catalogs, you'll save money—and enjoy a greater choice of plants—by raising perennials from seed. Start them in pots or a nursery bed; once they develop a set of true leaves, they are ready for the garden. Most perennials will bloom in about two years.

Most perennials require full sun and moist, well-drained soil. Select specimens that will thrive in your garden—whether it's boggy or dry, shaded or sunny, windblown or protected. Because perennials bloom for a brief period, select plants with attractive foliage.

If you need to cover an area quickly and economically, purchase perennials that reseed readily. Good self-sowers include yarrow, columbine, lamb's ears, bellflower, and pulmonaria. Also collect plant seed in fall and keep your eyes open for any volunteers for transplanting.

Some perennials bloom twice per season, either naturally or after being cut back. Among those to plant for a double dose of blooms are 'Miss Lingard' phlox, Siberian iris, snowdrop anemone, dwarf baby's breath, lythrum, and cranesbills.

Planting

A perennial will occupy its spot for many years, so plan carefully before you plant. Draw a small plan on graph paper. Arrange plants in combinations that show their flowers and foliage to best advantage, and remember that perennials look best when planted in drifts. Vary the number in each drift and intersperse with larger accent plants.

Hide the fast faders. Tuck plants whose foliage withers after blooming, such as poppies, bluebells, and bleeding heart, behind specimens that maintain their good looks, like Iberis, hosta, or lamb's ears.

When to plant: In regions with cold, wet winters or heavy soil, plant perennials in spring once the soil warms. Where winters are mild or soil is light, plant in autumn. Prepare the soil thoroughly, so the plants' long-lived roots will have a good home. Turn the soil over to at least 1 foot and incorporate plenty of organic matter to ensure good water and air circulation.

Maintenance

The most effective way to water perennials, which need about an inch of water weekly, is with a drip system or soaker hose. The soft stems may flop over if they are watered from above.

Mulch the beds year-round with an attractive organic mulch. It's the best way to suppress weeds, retain moisture, and prevent frost heaving over the winter.

Pinch them back. Keep perennials bushy and compact, and prevent tall stems from toppling by pinching out the stem tips.

Winterize your perennial garden by removing any dead flowers or foliage in autumn. After a hard freeze, cut back all stems to ground level and add extra mulch.

PESTICIDES

No garden is pest-free. But a well-tended garden contains a balance of beneficial predators and healthy, resistant plants—along with a tolerable number of undesirable insects and other pests. Use pesticides only if an infestation is causing damage and can't be otherwise controlled. Start with the least-toxic substance possible and move gradually to stronger measures as needed. Pesticides are generally sprayed or dusted on plants or soil. You must completely cover the affected plant or soil surface, including leaf undersides.

Pesticides are derived from a range of organic and synthetic sources, and are available in liquid or dry form. Many gardeners prefer organic types, which are made from bacteria, viruses, fungi, fatty acids, minerals, oils, and plants; they decompose quickly into nontoxic substances that won't harm the environment.

Systemic insecticides are absorbed by the plant and circulated by its sap, and can't be washed away by rain. Pests are killed when they feed on any part of the plant.

Be sure to identify the pest correctly and choose the appropriate pesticide. Many pesticides harm bees and other desirable insects. Try to use the most "specific" substance possible—one that targets the pest you want to destroy—and don't apply a bee-killing pesticide during bloom time, when bees are most active.

Horticultural oils, which include dormant oil and summer oil, are used to smother eggs and developing insects on trees and ornamentals. Use the heavier dormant oil in late winter or early spring, once temperatures are over 40°F, but before plants leaf out. Use the lighter summer oils any time the temperature is below 85°F.

Insecticidal soap is one of the best cures for soft-bodied pests like aphids, mites, and leaf miners. It is safe on most plants and is nontoxic to beneficial insects and animals. But don't spray it in direct sun, in extreme heat, or during drought.

Brew your own insecticidal soap by mixing 2 teaspoons dishwashing liquid with a few drops of vegetable oil and 1 gallon water. Use a plastic spray bottle to apply—but wash it thoroughly if it held household cleansers.

Some pesticides can scorch, discolor, or damage foliage. Always test the substance first on a small, inconspicuous part of the plant. Wait for a few days—if the growth remains healthy, use the pesticide on the entire plant.

Reserve a sprayer exclusively for pesticides; don't use it for herbicides or fungicides. Label it clearly with an indelible marker and clean it out thoroughly after each use.

Bottle it up! Prevent pets, birds, and children from touching a bait-type pesticide by placing it in a 1-pint plastic bottle. Bury the bottle in the ground so that its top is right at the soil line. Pests are small enough to crawl in and reach the bait, but critters and kids are not.

Using pesticides safely

Always read pesticide labels carefully and follow the directions on handling, use, and storage to the letter. Don't apply a pesticide to food crops unless the label states that it is safe to do so.

Apply pesticides on a dry, calm day with moderate temperatures and low humidity. Always keep children and pets away from pesticides while they're being applied and until they have dried or settled completely.

Cover as much of your skin as possible. Wear rubber gloves, a long-sleeved shirt, long pants, eye protection, and a dust mask. Never eat, drink, or smoke while handling pesticides. Avoid inhaling powders or sprays.

Clean all equipment carefully after application. Launder clothing separately.

Keep pesticides in their original packaging and store them in a secure, dry, cool place. Repeat applications only as needed and as indicated on the product label.

PETUNIAS

These indispensable annuals come in most solid colors and numerous bicolors that have contrasting veins, edges, center stars, or stripes. Petunias bear either single, trumpet-shaped blooms or ruffled double blooms. Of the two main types, grandifloras have fewer but larger flowers. Use them in hanging baskets, along paths, or in planters, where they will spill over the edges. Multifloras produce masses of smaller flowers and are more compact. Because they are more resistant to diseases, they are good for open borders and in humid climates.

Tiny petunia seeds need extra attention. About ten weeks before the last frost, sow indoors in a tray prepared with fine soil on top. Press the seeds well into the soil, but don't cover, and water from below. Plant out after danger of frost in soil amended with compost or rotted manure.

When seedlings are 6 inches tall, pinch the stem tips to encourage side branching.

Mulch petunias well so that mud won't splash up and mar the flowers when it rains.

Petunias get leggy in the middle of summer. Cut back the stems to 6 inches and give the plants extra fertilizer and water. Within a few weeks, they'll be blooming again.

Petunias are particularly susceptible to tobacco mosaic virus. If you smoke, do so away from the plants.

Look like rain? Then shield your petunias—even the sturdiest ones can be flattened by a downpour or a powerful squirt from the hose. Simply cover them with cardboard boxes or a plastic sheet draped over stakes to keep it off the plants.

PHOSPHORUS

Synthetic sources of phosphorus are superphosphate and diammonium phosphate. Organic sources include bonemeal, rock phosphate, and guano. Phosphorus moves downward in soil extremely slowly. When it is applied in liquid form to the surface, it remains at the top inch or so; in dry fertilizers, it remains near the granules. For this reason, make sure you apply phosphorus around the root zone.

Plants suffering from lack of phosphorus develop a bluish cast. Leaves may also turn a dark, dull green on top and bronze-purple on the undersides. Stems remain thin and may turn purplish. For a quick boost, spray plants weekly as needed with fish emulsion; it has about 5 percent phosphorus that is immediately available to plants.

Phosphorus becomes less available to plants in acidic and cold, wet soils. This is critical in spring, when young roots are trying to get established. Watch for symptoms of deficiency and add phosphorus as needed. You can also sweeten acid soil with wood ash to a pH of about 6.5 and warm it with black plastic mulch.

Bonemeal is a slow-release source of phosphorus, remaining in the soil for up to a year. Buy steamed, crushed bonemeal that is finely ground so that soil microorganisms can break it down more readily.

Rock vs. colloidal: Rock phosphate is washed, crushed limestone and contains about 33 percent phosphorus. It releases the nutrient slowly and will work in acidic soil. Collodial phosphate is the residue left from washing limestone and comes in small particles. It contains about 20 percent phosphorus, some of which is available immediately; it works best in neutral soil.

If you go overboard and end up with excess phosphorus, work in extra nitrogen and potassium to balance it out.

PINCHING

The terms "pinching," "pinching back," "pinching off," and "pinching out" are interchangeable. All refer to removing the growing stem tip or a bud—usually about ½ inch of growth—to spur compact, bushy plants and more buds.

For big blooms on dahlias, pinch out the side shoots to train it to a single stem. When buds appear, remove the lateral ones on the main cluster, leaving only the central bud. With chrysanthemums, start pinching out the stem tips when the plants are 8 inches tall and continue until mid-July, when the buds form. On rose standards, keep the trunk tidy and direct the energy to the top growth by pinching or cutting out any little buds that form along the stem. Eggplants and peppers often sprout many flowers that, if left alone, will make many small fruits. Pinch back some of the flowers so that the plant will expend its energy on producing larger fruits instead.

Pinching back can also help eliminate colonies of aphids. These common pests often cluster on the stem ends of beans, roses, and many ornamentals.

Variegated plants, with leaves marked in white, pink, or yellow, sometimes send out leaves of solid green. Pinch these back to the main stem; otherwise, the entire plant may revert to green.

Plants to pinch back

Ornamental plants: begonia, black-eyed Susan, bougainvillea, carnation, chrysanthemum, coleus, dahlia, fuchsia, helenium, impatiens, jade plant, marguerite, marigold, New York aster, nicotiana, pansy, peony, petunia, phlox, poinsettia, salvia, snapdragon, star jasmine, sweet pea, verbena, zonal geraniums. Edible plants: basil, beans, chervil, eggplant, grapes, melon, mint, oregano, peppers, pumpkin, rosemary, sage, squash, strawberry, tarragon, tomato.

PLANTING

Choose planting sites and prepare planting holes in advance. Make sure the location you choose meets the plant's cultural requirements and will permit the specimen to reach its mature height and spread.

Wait until the soil reaches at least 40°F before planting. Roots cannot grow in cold soil. Check the last frost date. Wait until the danger of frost has passed before planting out any tender specimens or young seedlings.

Don't rush to plant right after a rain—working soggy soil destroys its structure, and roots can rot in waterlogged soil.

Help young plants get off to a good start. Set them out on a cloudy day or in late afternoon so that the delicate leaves won't scorch. Keep them well watered until they're established.

Before setting out small plants in a windy or exposed area, first put the plant in a paper bag containing good soil. Then set the bag in the ground, leaving 2 inches of the rim above soil level. The seedling will be sheltered, and as it grows, the paper will decay and let the roots reach into the surrounding soil.

When setting out plants that have been grown in peat pots, rip off the rim and the bottom of the pot. Leave the rest intact; it will protect the roots and eventually break down in the soil.

Plant at the proper depth. Never set a plant significantly higher or lower in the soil than the depth at which it was previously grown. A notable exception is the tomato, which can be planted deeply; it produces new roots along the stems.

Never pull a plant out of its pot by the stem. Coax it out by running a knife around the inside of the container, staying close to the sides. Turn the pot on its side and tap the rim and base with a mallet. The plant should slide out easily. If not, break a clay pot with a hammer or cut open a plastic one with shears.

Loosen the roots of a container-grown plant before planting. Tease the roots apart with your fingers; if they are tightly wound, use a trowel or a kitchen fork. Place the plant in the hole and spread the roots in all directions before backfilling.

To eliminate air pockets when planting bare-root plants, make a mound of soil in the planting hole. Spread the roots out over the mound and fill in the hole halfway with soil. Add water to the top of the hole; let it drain out to settle the soil. Tamp lightly with your hands, then continue adding soil to the top of the hole. Water again and mulch.

POLLINATION

Pollination involves the transfer of pollen from the male stamen of the flower to the female pistil and results in the setting of seed. To produce fruit, many garden plants require pollination, which is generally done by insects, bees, and wind. Some plants, such as tomatoes and raspberries, can pollinate themselves; these are called self-fertile or self-pollinating. Self-sterile plants require pollination from another plant or another variety; examples of those needing cross-pollination include sweet cherries, pears, and most nut trees.

Check for compatibility. Always check with the nursery to see if the variety you want to grow as a pollinator is compatible with your other plants.

Make sure that your compatible plants will flower at the same time so that the pollen will be available.

Mix peas and beans. Plant some sweet peas (the flowers, not the veggies) near your pole beans. The plants will climb together, and pollinating insects attracted by the pea flowers will fertilize the beans.

Separate sweet and hot peppers. If cross-pollination occurs, you may find your sweet peppers become too hot to handle.

Shake your tomatoes. Even though tomatoes are self-fertile, they need help releasing their pollen. Just shake the plant or its stake to ensure the transfer of pollen.

If you're using a floating row cover to protect your vegetables from pests, remove it when the plants are in flower so that pollinating bees can do their work.

POPPIES

The poppy family *(Papaver)* includes fifty species of annuals and perennials with crinkled, cuplike blooms reminiscent of crepe paper. They come in numerous shades, both solid and bicolor, and in single or double form. Grow poppies in full sun in rich, very well-drained soil; standing water around the roots, especially in winter, can be fatal. Sow seed directly, since the poppy's long taproot makes it difficult to transplant.

For all the beauty of their blossoms, poppies have coarse, hairy foliage that some find unappealing; they also go dormant after bloom. Plant poppies behind other ornamentals that will shield their leaves and fill in the gaps once they fade.

POTASSIUM

Potassium, also called potash, is listed on fertilizer labels by its chemical symbol: "K." It's the third essential nutrient, indicated last in the N–P–K ratio. Potassium is required for proper growth of fruits and flowers, ensuring good size, color, and number. It helps plants build proteins and sugars and also aids plants in taking in other nutrients and withstanding the cold.

Plants need potassium when the leaves turn grayish, yellow, mottled, or brown, and the edges curl; lower stem leaves are affected first. Symptoms usually occur late in the season, when potassium is used by developing fruits. For a fast solution, spray plants with fish emulsion or liquid kelp. Or side-dress plants with wood ashes, which can contain up to 20 percent potassium.

Keep ashes dry. Almost all the potassium content will leach out of wood ashes when they are exposed to rain. Cover them with a tarp to keep them dry until use.

Root crops are heavy potassium users, so dig in a source of the nutrient before planting. But check on the plant's pH preference before using ashes, which lower acidity.

Discover langbeinite. This little-known mineral is a rich potash source, with about 22 percent potassium, 22 percent sulfur, and 11 percent magnesium—hence "sul-po-mag," its shorthand trade name.

Greensand and granite dust are good organic sources of potassium; both are slow acting and long lasting. Dig them into soil in fall so they'll be available when you plant in spring; they'll last for up to ten years.

The synthetic fertilizers potassium chloride (62 percent) and potassium sulfate (48 percent) are highest in potassium. Both act extremely fast.

POTATOES

Planting

Potatoes prefer cool weather and can't tolerate hot, dry soil. In areas with mild summers, grow long-maturing types. In hotter regions, you'll have better success with earlier varieties.

Never use potatoes grown the previous year for seed potatoes—they can harbor diseases. And don't plant store-bought spuds; they are usually treated with a sprouting inhibitor. Plant only certified disease-free seed potatoes, or "spud buds," from a reliable source.

If you live in a warm or hot climate, plant potatoes twice: in late winter for a spring crop and in late summer for a fall crop.

In cold climates, plant about four weeks before the last frost; the soil should be dry and at least 40°F. Plant early-, mid-, and late-season potatoes for a long harvest.

Loosen soil to a depth of a foot and incorporate about 2 pounds of compost for every 10 feet of row. Dig in 5–10–15 fertilizer a few days before planting. Count on harvesting about 4 pounds of potatoes per plant.

A bulb planter doubles as the perfect planting tool. Level the bed and make sure it is slightly moist. Make a hole 8 inches deep every 12 inches along the row (note that many planters are calibrated). Set in a piece of seed potato with three eyes: the indents where the sprouts grow. Then backfill the hole with soil from the bulb planter.

In heavy soil, plant potatoes in hills measuring 3 feet wide by 6 inches tall. Set the seed potatoes 6 inches apart around the center of the hill and cover with several inches of soil.

Maintenance

As plants grow, keep mounding soil or compost up around them to prevent sun from reaching the tubers. Light turns potatoes green and causes solanine, a mildly toxic substance, to develop.

Make sure you keep the soil moist, especially in warm weather. Provide 1 to 1 ½ inches of water weekly and mulch with compost or straw. Side-dress spuds with a little potassium nitrate when they reach 8 inches tall.

Keep diseases from the tubers by pulling off any infected leaves. To keep the tubers from being disturbed, place your feet astride the plant as you grab the leaves. Wait a week before harvesting the potatoes to make sure that no disease spores are still present. Prevent common scab, which disfigures the potato tubers, by keeping the soil slightly acid and well watered.

Harvesting

Harvest potatoes when the foliage withers and dies. Rub the tuber skin lightly with your finger; it should be firm and resist peeling.

Use a grub hoe to dig up your tubers—its wide, curved tines minimize the risk of injuring potato skins. Simply plunge it into the soil at the base of each hill and pull up.

Wait for a cloudy day. To prevent the formation of solanine and its telltale green coloration, don't expose the potatoes to sunlight when they are harvested or stored.

Cure potatoes for at least a week. Brush off the soil, but don't wash them, and spread them in a single layer in a dark place at around 60°F. Then store in a dry, dark, airy place with a temperature of 40°F. Check regularly for rotting potatoes and discard.

Tubers too sweet? If so, you may be storing them at too low a temperature.

POTTING MIXES

Potting soil usually contains equal parts loamy topsoil, sphagnum moss or peat moss, and either perlite, vermiculite, or sand. It should be clean and nutrient-rich.

Soilless potting mix is usually peat-based and also contains sphagnum moss, perlite, or vermiculite. Use it in planters when weight is a consideration or if a plant needs an especially light growing medium. Give plants grown in a soilless potting medium, such as peat moss, a lot of water and extra fertilizer. They need it.

Seed-starting mix has a light texture, retains water well, and is sterilized to prevent fungus diseases. Its main ingredients are soil, sand, and peat. It is low in nutrients.

Propagating mix is used for rooting cuttings and has peat, perlite, or sand as a base. It drains well but is nutrient-poor.

Planting mix generally refers to outdoor soil mixes for in-ground planting.

Specialized mixes contain ingredients that mimic conditions favored by certain plants, such as rock plants, azaleas, or orchids.

Compost is the name given to potting mix in some gardening books and magazines—especially those of British origin.

You don't necessarily have to repot a plant to keep its potting mix fresh. To give the soil new life, remove an inch or two from the surface of the old potting mix and use a fresh mixture to refill to the original level. You can also incorporate a slow-release fertilizer at the same time.

When preparing a potting mix, fill a heavy plastic trash bag halfway with the ingredients. Then close the bag and shake it at least ten times. To keep dust down, let the mixture settle for a few seconds before opening the bag.

Have a large pot? If so, you can make up the mix in place. Add each ingredient in small increments, mixing well with your hands each time.

Always make more potting mix than you need. Stored in a labeled plastic bag or a plastic bucket with a lid, organic mix will stay fresh for several months—and will come in handy for small planting tasks.

PRIMROSES

Most *Primula* species are called primrose, but this genus also includes the buttercup, oxlip, polyanthus, and cowslip. Primroses are usually listed in catalogs simply by the common species name, such as Japanese or English, while the polyanthus and pruhonicensis hybrids include many named cultivars. Choose species by their use and the kind of culture they prefer. Note the adaptability of the English primrose and the new hybrids.

Primroses prefer partial shade and cannot tolerate full sun in summer. They also need a cool spring, a mild summer, and consistently moist soil.

Early-flowering polyanthus primroses make fine companions for delicate spring flowers such as forget-me-nots and narcissus. The moisture-loving candelabra primrose, which flowers later, will look its best with ferns or astilbes or as an underplanting for rhododendrons.

Planting different strains of polyanthus primroses close together will result in seedlings of different colors next year; they hybridize easily. Although the new plants will bear little resemblance to their parents, they will still be attractive.

The drumstick, or Himalayan, primrose has round clusters of ½-inch lavender, purple, or white blossoms and is the first primrose to bloom in the spring. A rock garden favorite, it performs best when planted in the moist spaces between rocks, where the roots will remain cool.

If you live in a temperate region and can grow a deciduous woodland meadow, add English primroses and cowslips. Both are charmers in this setting and bloom in early spring.

In damp places, don't rush to remove the spent flowers of candelabra primroses. Left alone to set and spread their seed, they will colonize. In a few years, you'll have a collection of pink, crimson, and white flowers.

Don't be disappointed if the Japanese star primrose disappears in the summer. The plant dies down to avoid summer's heat—but will come back the following spring to bloom again. It is particularly lovely in dappled shade.

Old primroses with rhizomatous roots can be propagated by cutting off portions of the rhizomes in 2-inch lengths. Lay the cuttings horizontally in a box filled with peat and sand, covering them with the mixture about 3/8 inch deep. Keep them in a cold frame during the winter. The new plants will flower in the following season.

If you have patience, try starting different types from seed. Sow them in the fall in pots or small seed flats, then overwinter them in a cold frame. The cold period will break dormancy, and they should germinate in the spring. Keep in mind that fresh seed germinates more readily than old seed.

PROPAGATION

Propagating new plants is an inexpensive way to increase your garden stock. The most common method is to root cuttings, for which you need only a sharp knife, covered flats or pots, and rooting hormone powder. You can also propagate by layering, grafting, and dividing.

Reader's Digest Quintessential Guide

Propagation by cuttings simply involves removing part of a parent plant and rooting it. If cuttings are taken from healthy plants and have warmth, moisture, and a suitable growing medium, you can have new plants at very little cost.

The leaves left on cuttings are needed to nourish the developing roots, but too much foliage will demand more from the stem of the cutting than it can provide before the new roots begin to develop. Keep things balanced by removing the lower leaves and any flower buds. As the roots develop, new leaves will quickly appear. In the case of large-leaved plants, such as hydrangeas, it's a good idea to cut the leaves in half.

A do-it-yourself propagator: Fill an old plastic tray with soil and insert your cuttings. Remove the hooks from three coat hangers and bend the wires into hoops. Anchor the hoops in the soil at each end and in the middle of the tray. Then cover the tray with a clear piece of plastic, punching pinholes for ventilation.

Pot up cuttings quickly after the roots emerge. If the roots become entangled, separate them by gently immersing in a bucket of water and swishing them around.

The stems of some houseplants and half-hardy perennials, such as impatiens, will root in a glass of water. Cover the filled glass with a piece of aluminum foil and push the cuttings gently through, making sure that any leaves remain above the foil. Keep the water topped up and replace it completely if it turns green. When roots appear, pot the cuttings in very moist potting mix; cuttings rooted in water can be slow to thrive.

Make sure to trim your cutting with a very sharp knife or razor blade before you insert it into a potting medium. Ragged cuts can cause rotting.

Some plants with fleshy roots—including daylilies, sumac, and yucca—can be propagated from root cuttings. When the plant is fully dormant, lift it from the ground and cut back any top growth. Wash the roots, remove young ones (cutting them close to the crown), and return the parent plant to its original place in the garden. Cut 2-inch sections from the young roots and insert them in a pot filled with sandy potting mix, pushing them down until their tops are level with the surface. Do not water them until the shoots appear.

Heirloom, English, miniature, and many modern roses are good candidates for cuttings because they grow well on their own roots and don't necessarily need grafting. Pick healthy, new-growth stems after they have finished blooming. Cut with at least four leaflets intact. They will root in a few weeks.

Offsets: Bulbs and corms will form smaller offspring—tiny versions of themselves called bulblets or cormels. For narcissus and tulips, break off the offsets by hand and replant. For gladiolus corms, first let the corm dry out; then twist off the cormels. Store over winter and plant out in spring.

Cacti and succulents: To avoid rot, allow the base of any succulent cutting to dry or heal over before inserting it in a rooting medium—preferably cactus soil. The "chicks" of hens-and-chicks (echeveria) produce offshoots complete with their own roots. Simply break away the offsets and repot them in cactus soil.

Transplant cuttings to the planting bed on a rainy or overcast day. You'll minimize their shock of adapting to a new, sunny environment.

Success with cuttings

Practice first with a few easy cuttings. You'll have a high rate of success with asters, azaleas, camellias, chrysanthemums, coleus, forsythias, geraniums, hydrangeas, impatiens, ivy, oleanders, roses, and salvias.

Select parent plants that are vigorous growers and free of pests and disease.

Cut under a latent bud or node; this area contains more hormones and is more likely to produce roots.

Use a hormone rooting powder or solution, available at any garden center or nursery. Shake off the surplus; excess hormones may inhibit root development.

Provide excellent drainage: The more tender the cutting, the more sand the mixture must contain. The rooting mixture must be sterile.

Give bottom heat: 70°F for a herbaceous shoot or 55° to 60°F for a semihardwood cutting. Keep out of direct sun.

Maintain constant humidity—as close to 100 percent as possible.

PUMPKINS

Not just for pies. The pumpkin is one of the most versatile members of the gourd, or cucurbit, family. It is not only used for pies and soups but also has seeds that make tasty snacks when dried and roasted. But the pumpkin really comes into its own as a symbol of the witching season, when the plump orange fruits are transformed into Halloween jack-o'-lanterns.

Pumpkins love summer. Most varieties require about 110 frost-free days. In northern states it's best to start seed indoors, preferably under lights, three weeks before the last frost date. To ensure against frost damage after planting out, shield tender seedlings with a cloche or other protective device.

Direct sowing: After the last frost of spring, make shallow depressions in the soil and place five or six seeds in each one, spacing seeds 6 inches apart. When several true leaves have appeared, thin to two or three plants per hill. Pinch off the ends of the vines after a few fruits have formed.

Pest control. As soon as the seed is sown, it's a good idea to cover the row with a floating row cover. This will moderate the chancy spring weather and keep out the cucumber beetle, a serious pest.

Save space by growing pumpkins on a trellis. As they reach full size, they'll need support. An easy way is to slip them into old pantyhose and tie it to the lathes.

Don't lift by the stem when harvesting; if the stem breaks off, fungi and bacteria may enter, hastening spoilage. Wait until the vine dies to harvest—but remove the fruits immediately if frost threatens.

Cure harvested pumpkins for a week in a dry place at a temperature of about 75°F. To kill bacteria and fungi on the skin, dip the pumpkin in a weak chlorine solution (1 part bleach to 10 parts water). Store in an unheated attic away from dampness.

An old "Swamp Yankee" tip from New England says that pouring ½ cup of cream around each plant every three weeks gives the fruits a soft, creamy orange color.

QUINCE

With forsythia, the flowering quince (*Chaenomeles speciosa*) is one of the first shrubs to burst into bloom in the spring. It is grown for the ornamental value of both its flowers, which resemble apple blossoms, and its yellow fruits, which are fragrant but lack taste. The true quince (*Cydonia oblonga*) is a much larger plant grown mainly for its fruits, which can be cooked with meat or made into jelly.

Fruiting quince

The pear-shaped summer fruits of the popular 'Vranja' cultivar are preceded in late spring by white or pale-pink flowers. The fruits are golden yellow. The spreading tree grows to about 15 feet, as does the similar 'Lusitanica'.

Quince trees do best in good, moist loam but will survive in any garden soil. In colder climates, plant them in a sunny, sheltered corner. Keep the trees healthy and productive by working bonemeal (4 ½ ounces per square yard) into the surrounding soil in late winter. Apply a mulch of well-rotted compost in spring.

Watch out for blackened leaves and curled shoot tips on quince trees—a symptom of fire blight, which can kill the plant. Prune out infected parts only during the dormant season and dip your pruning shears into alcohol between cuts. Burn the infected prunings.

Harvest fruits of *C. oblonga* in fall before the first frost. By this time, they may be ripe and yellow or still green, depending on the variety. Store in a dry, frost-free place; within four to eight weeks, the green ones will ripen and turn yellow. Store quinces well away from other fruits, which can become tainted by their exceptionally strong aroma.

Flowering quince

To encourage a flowering quince bush to grow into a tree shape, allow only one stem to grow from ground level; this stem will become the future trunk. Cut away any low stems that try to grow. To grow flowering quince as a bush, let all of the stems grow more freely. As a freestanding bush, flowering quince needs only light pruning in the early summer to control its size.

Trim flowering quince, with its colorful blooms, into an eye-catching hedge. Its thorny branches also make it a natural barrier against intruders of the four-legged kind.

RADISHES

Radishes are often the first vegetables harvested in spring. Sow radish seed in with slow-germinating seed like that of carrots, beets, and Swiss chard. Quick to sprout, radishes will mark off the rows in a matter of days; make sure that you don't disturb the slower-germinating seeds while hoeing. The radishes will quickly be ready for harvest, freeing up space for the other crop.

Succession planting. Don't sow a whole packet of radish seed all at once. Ensure a longer harvest by sowing a third or a quarter of the packet every ten to fifteen days.

You can simply sow the seeds of round radishes on the soil surface. Long radish seeds, however, should be buried about ¾ inch deep to make sure that the roots grow long and are regularly shaped.

Encourage fast growth by giving radishes plenty of water; they can't tolerate drought conditions or heat waves. Sow them where they'll have partial shade at the hottest times of the day—planting near climbing beans or corn is ideal. If no shade is available, mulch the crop so that it stays cool. Or use a summer-weight floating row cover. The right conditions will result in crunchy radishes that aren't too peppery hot.

Fight turnip flies by protecting radish rows with a floating row cover. Only the early-maturing radishes, harvested in late April and the beginning of May, are safe from attack.

Don't throw away the tops. Rich in vitamins and minerals, radish greens have proven to be beneficial for the lower urinary tract. Harvest young greens only and add them to garden salads for a touch of peppery flavor. Mature radish greens should be used solely for soups.

RASPBERRIES

Thwart virus. Check at the nursery to make sure your new raspberry plants have been certified as virus-free. Don't let roots dry out before planting. Plant a few inches deeper than they were in their pots and cut them back to about 6 inches. Cultivate carefully; injured roots can admit virus.

To get a protective yet productive hedge, mix single-crop and double-crop raspberries with blackberries. Add a climbing vine like trumpet honeysuckle to lace the canes together. The plants create a prickly barrier while providing a season-long berry harvest.

Too little space? Tie two raspberry bushes around a stake about 5 feet tall. Gather the branches together gently with strips of soft cloth, making sure to leave space between the canes for air circulation.

To prune June-bearing single-crop varieties, cut the second-year canes, which have borne fruit and are turning brown and dry, to the ground. At the same time, cut back any first-year canes that have yet to bear fruit to a height of about 4 feet; these will branch out and produce fruit the following year. To prune everbearing raspberries, cut all canes that have borne fruit back to 4 feet.

To keep long canes from touching the ground or blowing about in the wind, build a support. Drive sturdy posts 2 to 2 ½ feet into the ground, then stretch wire between them at knee- and chest-height. There is usually no need to attach the canes to the wires.

Watch for dry spells, which can decrease the crop and the size of the berries. Keep your raspberry bushes well irrigated at such times, watering in the evening.

Probable pests: Japanese beetles love raspberries; pick off the pests and crush them. Aphids can be controlled by a heavy spray from a garden hose or an application of insecticidal soap. Spray fruit worms, which eat the buds, with carbaryl or rotenone.

Raspberries are also vulnerable to many diseases, especially in warm climates. Pick up any canes that are diseased or winter-killed, and burn them. Remove nearby wild bramble bushes to allow air to circulate freely.

Don't discard hard, dry raspberry bush canes after you've pruned them off. They will become excellent kindling for your fireplace.

RHODODENDRONS

The genus *Rhododendron* encompasses a huge variety of plants—both deciduous and evergreen, from tree-size to dwarf. Rhododendrons are distinguished by their handsome foliage and glorious blooms in a variety of colors. Although most rhododendrons measure between 5 and 8 feet tall when mature, some varieties have enormous flowers and can grow as high as 80 feet in the wild. Other species, like *Rhododendron yakusimanum* and its cultivars, are dwarf shrubs perfectly suited for containers and rock gardens.

Planting

Rhododendrons prefer acidic, moist, well-drained soil. Dig a hole twice as wide and deep as the root-ball and toss a couple of handfuls of gypsum into the planting hole to promote drainage—especially in clayey soil. Mix the backfill thoroughly with well-rotted manure, peat moss, or compost. Make sure to put plenty of this nutritious mix in the top foot of soil, where the roots tend to grow.

Remove the burlap. While you can install some balled-and-burlapped plants with the natural burlap left around the root-ball, it is not recommended for rhododendrons. The fabric can wick moisture away from the shallow roots. What's more, some "burlap" contains synthetic fibers that don't decompose and can inhibit root growth.

Soil too heavy? If so, plant rhododendrons in a raised bed or a mound. When mounding, cover the root-ball completely with soil and mulch just to the crown.

Though most rhododendron species can be propagated from cuttings, some of the large-leaved species can take up to six months. Take cuttings from new growth, treat with a rooting hormone, and insert into a peat container of potting soil. Place under glass and mist frequently to maintain 100 percent humidity. Don't overheat: Place the cuttings out of the sun. Plant out the following spring.

Semishade is more suitable than full shade for rhododendrons, since exposure to sun for about half the day promotes abundant flowering. On the other hand, too much scorching sunlight and dryness at the roots are detrimental.

Avoid competition. Don't plant rhododendrons near surface-rooting trees, like birches, elms, and poplars. Both trees and rhododendrons will suffer from the ensuing competition between their roots. Deep-rooting trees, such as oaks, pines, and dogwoods, won't compete with rhododendrons.

Maintenance

Because rhododendrons have shallow feeder roots, cultivate around them with extreme care. Spread 2 to 3 inches of mulch to prevent weeds. Also use mulch to retain moisture and shield the roots from heat and sun.

Feed planting beds with acid-forming fertilizer. Use compost made from materials that become acidic as they decompose. When mulching, use an acidic mulch of pine needles, shredded pine bark, or shredded oak leaves.

Water well during dry spells. Rhododendrons like moisture and won't tolerate drought for prolonged periods. Water thoroughly if it hasn't rained for ten to fourteen days, but don't let the soil become soggy. Refrain from watering heavily late in the season; this may promote new growth too tender to withstand winter freezes.

Drooping leaves in warm weather may indicate root rot (while rhododendrons crave moisture, their roots can't tolerate standing water). To save the plant, dig it up, gently shake the dirt from its root-ball, and put it in the shade for several days, letting the roots dry out. Remove damaged roots that have turned black. Before replanting, redig the hole and discard the soil. Or dig a new hole; slash the sides of the hole with the shovel, dig in a couple of handfuls of gypsum to promote drainage, and use garden soil amended with compost or well-rotted manure for the backfill.

Deadhead gently. Remove the spent blossoms as soon as possible so that the plant expends its energy on forming next year's buds, not seeds. Either snap the clusters off with your fingers or nip them with shears. Be careful: The tiny flower and leaf buds are located right beneath the old flower head. If you injure them, there will be no growth the following year.

Rhododendrons don't need regular pruning, although you can prune young specimens lightly to encourage a bushy shape. Keep in mind, however, that rhododendrons won't produce new growth below a cut where no buds or shoots are visible along the branch. Always cut back just to a bud, which is found right above the leaf cluster.

If an old rhododendron has grown leggy or sparse, remove lower branches to form more of a tree shape. Lop branches off at the stem and lightly prune some of the top growth. Keep the plant well mulched and watered, since the roots will be exposed to more sunlight and heat.

Underplant your rhododendrons with low-growing, shade-loving woodland perennials like creeping phlox, foamflower, trillium, and ferns. They will not only keep roots cool but also provide a colorful carpet.

Keep your rhododendron alive with color by planting a large-flowered hybrid clematis, such as 'Nellie Moser' or 'Niobe', to climb up through its branches and adorn the shrubs after the rhododendron blooms fade.

Leaching lime: If you plant near a house or foundation made of brick and mortar, the soil around rhododendrons will eventually become more alkaline as lime leaches from the building. Compensate by treating the soil with peat moss, ferrous sulfate, or other acid-forming material.

First aid for cold damage: Wrap a rhododendron's splitting bark with strips of cloth to encourage the shrub to repair the damage. Ridge up a generous layer of mulch around the base of the plant.

RHUBARB

A well-tended rhubarb plant, started from seed or a root crown, can be harvested for fifty or more years. For a hearty harvest, prune off rhubarb flowers as soon as they form. The ornamental spikes—prized for their beauty by some gardeners—draw nutrients from the stalks.

Rhubarb stalks are ready to pull when they are 1 to 1½ feet long. The newly developing stalks of the deepest red usually have the best flavor. Pulling season is over when emerging stalks stay small.

When harvesting, never cut a rhubarb stalk off the plant. The remaining stub will bleed and invite rot. Instead, hold the stalk near the base and give it a slight twist as you pull it away.

When transplanting cabbage family plants, slip a few slices of rhubarb into soil near the roots. The oxalic acid in rhubarb can check the growth of the cabbage-harming fungi that are common in poorly drained or acidic soil.

Eat rhubarb stalks only. Trim off the leaves well below the leaf joint. Rhubarb leaves contain high levels of oxalic acid, which can contribute to kidney problems in susceptible people.

To take the acidic bite out of rhubarb, soak peeled stalks in cold water for several hours. Or blanch them in boiling water before cooking.

ROOTING HORMONES

Propagation with plant cuttings is more successful when you use a synthetic rooting hormone, which works like a plant's natural hormones. Hormone powders come in varying strengths—weak ones for softwood and herbaceous stems and strong ones for hardwood cuttings.

A homemade version: Willows give off indolebutyric acid, a natural rooting hormone. Soak pieces of willow bark in rainwater for two days and water cuttings with the solution. It doesn't keep, so make it fresh as needed.

Don't overdo it. Too much hormone powder can cause rot. To avoid overdosing, stick the base of a cutting into the powder and then tap it with your finger to knock off the excess.

Rooting rhododendrons: Certain large-leaved species of rhododenron, including *R. minus* 'Scintillation', are fairly difficult to propagate; roots form in the stem and are then stopped by the bark layer, which is sensitive to hormones. To remedy, make a vertical wound on one side of the cutting with a grafting knife, lift or remove the flap of bark, and treat only the exposed stem with hormone powder. Roots will grow from the callus tissue around the wound.

ROSEMARY

A Mediterranean native, rosemary makes a good shrub in Southern California and climates with dry summers and mild winters. Its hardiness in other warm and hot climates depends on light protection; cold, dry winds will quickly dehydrate the leaves. In cold and temperate areas, rosemary is best grown in pots.

Light, well-drained soil is essential for rosemary, especially for container-grown plants; waterlogged soil will cause woodiness and death. Plants also need full sun. Feed in only very poor soils, and lightly.

Fast growing and tough, rosemary is ideal for simple topiary shapes. To make a tree, choose a plant with a straight central stalk. Prune the lower branches repeatedly until the plant reaches the desired height (you can use the cuttings in cooking). Count on 4 to 4 ½ feet of growth in two years. Then trim the head into a ball, cone, or any shape you like. Clip rosemary anytime except during periods of stress caused by temperature extremes.

Tossing rosemary sprigs on the coals or grate of the barbecue during the last ten minutes of cooking imparts a wonderful flavor and aroma to lamb, veal, or chicken. Rosemary branches can be used as shish kebab sticks; they can also be tied together to make an aromatic brush for applying sauce to the meat as it cooks.

ROSES

Modern roses are hybrids that combine the winter hardiness of wild northern species with the lush everblooming habits of their southern relatives. Hybrid tea roses produce large individual flowers; floribundas bear blossoms in clusters. Climbing roses, despite the name, need to be tied to a support. Most roses grow best where they get at least six hours a day of direct sun.

Planting

Bushes are usually shipped bare-root. Just before planting, rehydrate roots by soaking them in a bucket of water overnight. If you can't plant right away, open the container and moisten the roots. Reclose and store it for up to two weeks in a cool, dark place where the temperature stays an even 35° to 40°F.

Nursery-bought roses are already planted in pots or boxes. So as not to disturb the roots, cut out the bottom of the container and set the still-packaged root-ball into the planting hole. Slit one side of the container and gently remove it before backfilling the hole with soil or compost enriched with peat moss.

A drainage test: Dig a hole 18 inches deep at the desired planting spot and fill it with water. If the water is gone within two hours, the site is suitable for roses. If water is still standing after two hours, build a raised bed for your bushes.

In northern gardens, plant grafted nursery-bought rose bushes deep to protect the graft union from winter cold. Make sure the union is 1 or 2 inches below the soil surface.

In southern gardens, plant nursery-bought roses so that the graft union sits an inch or more above ground level. This placement discourages the cultivated canes from forming their own roots and rejecting the grafted ones.

Good company: Planted near rose bushes, lavender drives away aphids; sage, hyssop, and thyme deter caterpillars; French marigolds may discourage nematodes. For spring color, plant early bulbs such as narcissus, grape hyacinth, or crocus under the roses. The plants will bloom and go dormant before the rose leaves can shade them.

Orientation: Canes on a new rose bush sprout mainly from one side of the bud union. To produce a well-shaped mature bush, place the new rose in the planting hole with the sprouting side facing north. Equal growth on the other side of the bush will be stimulated by its southern exposure.

Maintenance

In hot, dry weather, roses need an inch of water a week, either from rain or the hose. Use a bubbler (available at garden centers) on the hose so that the water seeps into the soil around the rose's roots without wetting foliage; damp leaves will invite fungus diseases.

To keep modern hybrid tea and floribunda roses blooming throughout the growing season, remove fading flowers before the seeds, or rose hips, can form. As the petals start to drop, cut off the flower just above the fourth leaf cluster; ideally, the cluster should be outward-facing, with five leaflets. A new flowering stem will sprout from the base of the topmost remaining leaf.

Climbing roses will flower more profusely if you train them to follow a horizontal line along a trellis or frame while the canes are still young and supple. Forming an arch by fastening the end of a cane to a peg in the ground will encourage even more blooms.

To stimulate the continued flowering of everblooming roses throughout the summer, drench the roots of each bush with 2 to 4 tablespoons brewer's yeast dissolved in 2 gallons water immediately after the first blooming.

When rose varieties are grafted onto another rootstock

variety, the rootstock will occasionally send out vigorous shoots. These undesirable shoots, or suckers, should be pruned out, as they can eventually choke out the parent plant.

Yellowed leaves with dark-green veins are a symptom of chlorosis, a condition caused by an iron deficiency. Apply a fertilizer containing chelated iron, but first test your soil: To keep iron from "locking up," the soil's pH must be between 5.5 and 6.5. If the pH is higher, apply sulfur; if lower, apply lime.

Propagation: Take cuttings in June from a vigorous pencil-thick cane; one bearing a bloom is at the right stage of maturity. Cut the cane into 6- to 8-inch lengths, making sure that each one has at least three leaves. Without damaging the buds at their bases, trim off all but the top leaf on each. Cut a cross into the base of each cutting with a sharp knife and slip a grain of rice into the center of the cut. To keep the grain in place, bind the cutting's base (but not too tightly) with twine. Stand the cutting in water overnight, then pot it in a mix of equal parts sand and soil. Water the pot thoroughly and set it in a cool and bright but shaded spot. Keep each pot well watered. The cuttings should root in two or three weeks.

For the cleanest, least traumatic cuts on rose canes, use a sharp pair of bypass, or scissors-type, pruning shears; anvil-type shears can do damage. To prune the largest canes on your bushes, use long-handled lopping shears.

Timing: Modern everblooming roses, such as hybrid teas and floribundas, are pruned to best effect in early spring, just as the leaf buds swell. Roses that flower once a year should be pruned just after blooming.

Prune everbloomers by removing any dead or damaged canes. Then take out any canes that grow in toward the center of the bush and any that cross and rub each other. Cut off the suckers that sprout from below the graft union. Choose three to six of the strongest canes to keep, and cut all the other canes off at ground level. Then trim the remaining canes to the desired height.

Prune once-blooming roses as you would any flowering shrub to create an open, balanced framework of sturdy branches. To keep the growth compact, cut back each cane by a quarter.

Rake up pruned clippings and dispose of them, since they may harbor disease spores or insect eggs and larvae. For the same reason, rake up and dispose of fallen rose leaves in autumn.

At the first sign of black spot—a common leaf disease for roses in humid weather—mix 2 teaspoons baking soda and a few drops of liquid soap with 1 gallon of water. Spray the whole bush with the mixture. Reapply the mixture every four or five days until the spots disappear and the weather becomes drier.

Standard roses, often called tree roses, are actually rose bushes grafted onto long rootstock trunks. To protect the graft union over the winter, simply cut off the sleeve of an old sweater or sweatshirt. Prune back the rose's top growth in late fall so that you can slip the sleeve over the branches and around the graft union on the trunk below. Then stuff the sleeve with peat moss, dry leaves, or straw for insulation; tie a plastic bag over it to keep out ice and snow. Remove the sleeve in early spring.

SAGE

Like many Mediterranean herbs, garden sage (*Salvia* spp.) loves sun and well-drained soil. Water young plants well, then keep on the dry side. In humid heat, try a gravel mulch to keep roots cool. Catalogs often describe sages as short-lived perennials or half-hardy annuals. In fact, some "annuals" may survive mild winters, while extreme cold or hot, humid conditions may kill some "perennials." In cold areas, prune plants in the spring to shape them and remove dead growth. In most southern gardens, it's best to treat sage as an annual.

Cut fresh sprigs as needed. For drying, cut off no more than a third of any individual plant. Strip leaves and lay them out on paper towels until dry. Store in a dark, tightly sealed container.

Garden sage has a variety of culinary uses. Place a few sprigs under a roast before putting it in the oven. Sprinkle some chopped leaves on a pizza before adding toppings or use in cheese dishes. Also put young leaves in vegetables, salads, and soups. Sage tea has an honorable history as an antiseptic mouthwash and digestive aid. Indeed, an old adage holds that "no man need be ill if sage grows in his garden."

Ornamental sages, including scarlet salvia and silver sage, are used only for decorative purposes. If growing the former, be aware that its brilliant red color looks best against a palette of green leaves, rather than mixed with such vibrantly colored plants as marigolds and zinnias.

For wreaths and arrangements, cut back flowering stems of garden sage. Secure a bunch with a rubber band and hang it upside down in a cool place to dry.

SALAD GREENS

Plant salad greens in good, well-drained soil—preferably in raised beds. Cool-season crops need especially good drainage around their roots, which can easily rot. Or plant a hanging basket with salad greens and herbs for a cook's garden right outside the kitchen door. It's out of reach of slugs and caterpillars, too.

Use a fine sifter to evenly distribute potting soil or sterile germinating mix over the tiny seeds of most greens.

In cool climates, make successive sowings of salad crops from March to October. Plant each new row as the first reaches about an inch in height. In warm climates, plant in fall after the nights cool; greens will grow through a mild winter. If nights get too cool in early spring or late fall, protect crops from frost and wind with floating row covers.

Scorching sun harms leafy greens, causing many to bolt or taste bitter. As heat increases, water more regularly and cover plants with shade netting over wire hoops.

Create your own version of the gourmet mixture called mesclun from leftover seed packets of lettuce, chicory, escarole, chervil, garden cress, and arugula. Sow them densely and harvest the leaves when young and tender.

Uniform moisture is the secret to regular growth and crisp, well-formed leaves. Mulch plants with a layer of straw or hay and keep them well watered.

Harvest the leaves from your greens often. Be sure to pick them from the outside so that the young inner leaves will keep growing and developing.

SEEDS

Stratification and scarification make it possible to speed the germination of certain seeds.

Stratification is the name given to the process of inducing seeds to emerge from dormancy through cold treatment. To stratify, soak the seeds for up to twenty-four hours and combine them with a mix of moist peat and sand in a plastic bag. Place the mixture in the refrigerator and keep at a temperature of 34° to 41°F for four to twelve weeks.

Seeds to stratify: aconite, bells of Ireland, bleeding heart, columbine, cotoneaster, daylily, euonymus, gas plant, hellebore, hickory, holly, juniper, lavender, *Lathyrus* spp., lupines, *Meconopsis* spp., peony, phlox, primula, species roses, serviceberry, trillium, *Viola* spp.

Some seeds have hard coverings that must be penetrated before they will germinate. This treatment—called scarification—can be done in one of two ways, depending on the size of the seed. Large seeds can be nicked with a sharp file or rubbed with fine sandpaper or an emery board until the coat is broken; this is where the new sprout will start. Seeds too small to nick are soaked overnight in a hot-water bath. Place the seeds in a container and pour water heated to about 190°F over them, in a water-to-seed ratio of 6:1. After twenty-four hours, remove the seeds and sow immediately without drying.

Seeds to scarify: apple, beans, beets, canna, carrots, celery, honey locust, impatiens, laburnum, lupin, mimosa, morning glory, pansy, parsley, peas, stone fruits, sweet peas.

To test old seed for viability, pour it into a glass of water. Seeds that fall to the bottom have a good chance of growing. Discard those that float to the top.

Another test: Place thirty-odd seeds left over from last year's packet between two moist paper towels for a few days. Remoisten the towels often and lift a corner to check for germination. Use the percentage of germinated seed as a guide for how much to sow.

The tops of water heaters or refrigerators make a perfect place to set a seed flat if their temperature matches that needed for germination—75°F for asparagus, lettuce, and peas, for example.

To protect gathered seeds from many of the various fungal and bacterial diseases, soak them in hot water (125°F) for thirty minutes. Coating seeds with a small amount of a fungicide, like captan, helps deter damping off.

When collecting seeds in the wild, always leave enough seed on the plant so that it can continue developing in its native habitat.

Most seed packets contain more seed than you can use in one season. To store for the following year, carefully fold over the tops of packets and place in a plastic or wooden file box. Use index cards or dividers to categorize the seeds.

SLUGS AND SNAILS

These gastropod gourmands take a special liking to the following: dahlias, delphiniums, hostas, lupines, marigolds, zinnias, and almost any flower or vegetable seedling. Plants that are reputed to repel snails include azaleas, apricot, basil, beans, California poppies, corn, chard, daffodils, fennel, fuchsias, grapes, ginger, holly, parsley, Peruvian lily, pumpkins, plum, rhododendrons, rhubarb, sage, and Swedish ivy.

The infallible beer trap: Slugs and snails find the yeast in beer irresistible. Bury a container half filled with the brew where they can easily climb into it and die; the alcohol destroys their body tissue. Dump the container and add new beer every day.

A sugar shack: Dissolve a teaspoon each of jam, sugar, and lemon juice in a glass of water; pour the mixture into a can with two or three openings cut in the side; push the sharp metal edges inward. Attracted by the sweets, slugs will climb in and be killed by the acidic lemon juice.

Protect young plants by encircling them with a sandpaper collar. Either cut your own or use a sandpaper collar for a drill disc; the rough surface will discourage the soft-bodied pests.

Barriers of sand or ash should be several inches deep and encircle the plant entirely. During periods of severe slug infestation, avoid mulching plants with straw, leaves, compost, or other organic materials. In addition to hiding in these mulches, the pests will likely lay their eggs there.

Slugs and snails are nocturnal. After dark, hunt in their favorite feeding places, armed with a flashlight and a saltshaker or a bucket of salty water. Salted slugs and snails don't survive.

Upturned half-grapefruit rinds can serve as lethal traps before being discarded; the juice is acidic.

SOIL

The most fundamental element in the garden is soil: the very foundation for all plants. The gardener's job is to see to it that soil is healthy and in the best possible condition.

Evaluating soil

Soil is made up of inorganic particles—sand, silt, and clay—as well as organic matter, air, and water. Soil quality depends on the proportion of these components and the activity of the attendant microorganisms, earthworms, and fungus.

Acidity and alkalinity in soil are measured on the pH scale, which runs from 0 (pure acid) to 14 (pure alkaline). From the neutral point of 7.0, the numbers increase or decrease geometrically: Thus a pH of 5.0 is 10 times more acid than a pH of 6.0. For a quick pH test, buy litmus paper, sold at most pharmacies; it should come with a color scale. Mix distilled water and soil in a clean cup until a moist paste forms. Then insert the litmus paper. To find the pH, match the paper's final color to the scale.

Analyze structure and texture. Texture refers to the amount of sand, silt, and clay in the soil, while structure refers to how the components clump together. To test structure, rub a pinch of moist soil between thumb and forefinger. Soil that's too sandy feels gritty. Silty soil feels smooth and slick, while clayey soil feels sticky and rolls up easily. For ideal "loam," with a mealy feel, the soil should contain up to 50 percent sand, between 25 and 50 percent silt, and up to 25 percent clay.

A texture test: Lightly squeeze a handful of moist soil. If the clump crumbles apart, the soil is sandy. If it forms a sticky ball, it is clayey. If the soil ends up as a spongy ball, you have loam.

Test for tilth, which refers to the soil's fitness for cultivation. Drop a spadeful of moist soil on a hard surface: If it breaks into small crumbs, the soil has good tilth and is ready for planting. If the soil breaks into clods, it is too heavily compacted and needs amending.

Rich or lean? A "rich" soil teems with thirteen of the nutrients plants need for growth, including trace elements. "Lean" or "light" refers to a soil that is low in fertility.

Managing soil

Don't walk on, work in, or drive machinery over wet soil. Also refrain from excessive tilling. Doing either can damage soil structure, compacting the pores so that air and water won't be able to move through.

The single most important way to improve all soils is by adding organic matter. Work 1 to 4 inches of rotted manure, compost, chopped leaves, or other source into the soil each year to produce rich, crumbly humus. Turn it in deeply: Digging or tilling the soil adds oxygen, which microorganisms need to break down organic matter and release nutrients.

SPINACH

Heat makes spinach bolt. In warm and hot climates, plant in the fall for harvests in winter and early spring. In cold and temperate areas, plant a spring crop as soon as the soil can be worked or anytime before daytime temperatures reach 70°F; start a fall crop in August. To overwinter, use row covers or straw mulch.

Spinach matures quickly, needing only about forty days until harvest. Sow short rows every two weeks to ensure a steady supply of tender young leaves.

Help spinach stay cool by planting it at the base of corn, squash, beans, or peas—any tall or trellis-grown plant that will block out some of the sun but still allow for good air circulation.

Sow shallow. Place seeds ¼ inch deep and 1 inch apart in a neutral soil enriched with compost or manure; thin to between 3 and 6 inches apart when seedlings reach 1 inch tall. Instead of discarding the tiny plants, add them to a salad.

Keep plants well fed and watered. Fertilize with 1 tablespoon fish emulsion mixed with 1 gallon water. Use about 1 cup per 1-foot row once the leaves emerge and feed weekly until plants are 3 inches tall, then feed a few more times during the season. Provide constant moisture to keep spinach from bolting.

Look for leaf miners, whose larvae tunnel inside the spinach leaves. If you find trails on the leaves or eggs underneath, pick and destroy the foliage; don't compost it. Treat plants with pyrethrin and till the bed under at season's end.

Cut or pinch the leaves to harvest instead of pulling them. Once the central seed stalk forms with the warmer weather, cut the whole plant back to the soil line.

SQUASH

Squash are ancient indigenous food crops and comprise two distinct types. Summer squash are bushy plants with soft-skin fruits. Winter squash grow on vines and have a hard rind. All squash like rich soil and plenty of sunshine.

Prepare for planting by digging a hole large enough to hold a bushel of cow manure or compost; dump it in and top off with 3 inches of good garden loam. Don't place where squash and its relatives have been grown in the past year or so. Interplant with radishes or basil to repel borers and beetles.

For best germination, sow seed when the soil temperature is 60°F or above.

There's no need to feed. If you've amended the soil with manure, don't add fertilizer during the growing season. If not, incorporate a 5–10–10 at planting time and side-dress each plant when it starts to vine.

Black plastic mulch isn't pretty, but squash love it anyway. Use it to raise soil temperature, conserve moisture, reduce weeds, and deter pests.

Place aluminum foil under squash plants to reflect light and confuse the squash borer moth, who lays her eggs at the base of the stem. If you do see eggs, simply scrape them off. The squash species *Cucurbita moschata*, which includes the 'Butternut' variety, is resistant to borers.

Minimize mildew by allowing for good air circulation. At the first sign of fungus, spray with a solution of 1 teaspoon baking soda mixed in 1 quart water; add ¼ teaspoon cooking oil or soap to help it stick.

Don't be alarmed if some of the flowers don't set fruit. Squash produce male and female flowers on the same plant, but only the females bear fruit after being pollinated by bees. You'll recognize the females by their short stems and a small bulge—the young squash—below the vase-shaped blossom.

Summer squash: Yellow crookneck and straightneck, zucchini, and scallop (also called pattypan) squash are notoriously prolific. Plan on only one plant per person. Plant in rows, sowing about three seeds per foot, then thin to 18 inches apart. The close spacing reduces yield per plant but will increase it per square foot. Harvest when it is still immature—no more than 6 inches long, with tender skin. Do the thumbnail test: The skin should be soft and easily pierced when pressed. Pick regularly to encourage productivity.

Winter squash: plant in hills, sowing five seeds in each and thinning to the best three seedlings. Be sure to allow at least 6 to 8 feet around the hill for the vines to spread. To save space, pinch off the vine ends after enough fruit has set and turn the tips of the vines back toward the hill. Or train the plants on a trellis or tripod, supporting the fruits in a sling of pantyhose or soft cloth—perhaps an old bedsheet. Keeping them off the ground also exposes the fruits to more sun, prevents rotting, and makes harvesting easier. Harvest once the rinds are firm and the vines begin to shrivel. Cut the stem about 2 inches above the fruit. While no squash is frost hardy, don't worry about cool fall nights—they bring out the sugars in the flesh and produce the sweet flavor. If the fruit has not quite matured by harvest time, cure it at 80°F for about ten days. Then wash the rind with a solution of 1 part chlorine bleach to 10 parts water, dry, and store in a cool dark place; they will last for several months. Check often for soft spots—a sign of rot.

STRAWBERRIES

Purchasing

How much is enough? For a family of four, plant about a dozen June-bearing strawberries, which fruit only once, and a dozen everbearing types, which produce crops in spring and late summer. Each plant yields from a cup to a pint per year.

Check the neck. Whether you're buying bare-root plants in spring or potted ones any time in season, look for a healthy, rot-free crown, or neck, where the flower buds and fruits will form. Spotless green leaves and whitish roots also indicate plant vigor.

Guard against virus by buying certified disease-free stock; strawberries are particularly susceptible to diseases. Always select varieties adapted to your area.

Planting

Strawberries like rich, acidic, and well-drained soil. In early spring, prepare a thoroughly tilled, well-weeded bed amended with plenty of humus, compost, or aged manure.

Blanket the bed four to eight weeks before planting time with a sheet of black or clear plastic mulch. The heat of sunlight will "solarize" the soil, inhibiting weed growth. To plant, slice crosses in the covering 12 to 18 inches apart and set in the plants.

Overcast days are the best time to plant, even though strawberries love the sun; they will be less stressed. Soak their roots in water for several hours beforehand.

Strawberries are fussy about their depth in the soil. Plant so that the crown is just above grade. If planted too deep, the plants will rot; if too shallow, they'll dry out. To make sure that the plants are set at the proper depth, water in thoroughly and note any settling of the soil. If the crowns sink, dig up the plants and raise; if they are protruding, add more soil to cover. Check again after the first rainfall.

To help strawberries develop a strong root system, dig a hole about 6 inches wide and a few inches deeper than the roots. Mound soil in the center of the hole and spread the roots evenly over the top. If the roots are too long, never fold them up; snip with scissors instead.

Keep strawberries close at hand for munching by planting them in containers for the terrace. If you don't have an actual strawberry pot, use any tub or barrel with holes in its sides, where you can tuck in plants. To water evenly, insert a perforated pipe down the center of the pot; it can be left in or filled with gravel, which stays in place when the pipe is pulled out.

Keep moving. Once an existing strawberry bed becomes less productive, start a new one in another part of the garden. But don't choose a spot where tomatoes, peppers, or potatoes have been grown in the last three years; strawberries are prone to the same soilborne diseases that attack these vegetables.

Maintenance

After the first flowering, mulch with straw, shredded pine bark, or pine needles to keep fruits from touching the soil. You can also use plastic collars.

Strawberries need to be kept moist. But take care: Water only in the morning so that the plants can dry before sundown.

Get young plants off to a good start and ensure bountiful harvests in succeeding years by pinching off the flower buds the first season. With June-bearing strawberries, this means forfeiting fruit; on everbearing plants, removing the buds through July 1 stimulates the late-summer crop.

Feed in summer by digging in compost enriched with blood meal and hoof-and-horn meal; use about 2 to 3 bushels per 100 square feet. Add a little nitrogen-rich fertilizer if you notice that the leaves are yellowing.

Reader's Digest Quintessential Guide

Speed the harvest. Strawberries will ripen and be ready to pick sooner if you protect the beds with plastic tunnels or row covers very early in spring.

Pick strawberries when they are still about 25 percent white. They'll turn berry-red in a day, and you'll avoid the risk of having overripe fruit rot on the vine if rain delays harvesting. For best flavor, always take the whole stem and handle the tender fruits gently to minimize bruising.

Store ripe berries unwashed in the refrigerator; wash and remove the stems and caps only just before using. Wet strawberries spoil quickly, even if kept chilled.

Thwart thieving birds by stretching nets over the rows when the berries begin to redden. You can also set up wires that whir in the wind; twist the wires slightly so that they vibrate and "sing" even louder.

As strawberries age, they weaken, falling prey to diseases and pests. Each year, pull out and destroy the oldest plants and add an equal number of new ones in fresh soil. With June-bearing types, you can also renovate your strawberry bed immediately after harvest by burning off the old foliage or clipping it 3 inches above the crown.

Examine plants regularly for signs of insect infestation or disease, and treat accordingly. Red, yellow, or purple foliage may indicate aphids, spider mites, mildew, or a virus. A fuzzy mold on fruits is a fungus.

Help young runners put down roots by pinning them directly to the soil with 4-inch lengths of wire bent in a *U* shape around a broom handle held in a vise. You can also bury 3-inch pots in the soil at grade level and peg the runners over them. Cut the runner from its parent six weeks later and wait another week to transplant it in fresh soil.

In areas with hard freezes, mulch after the first frost with several inches of straw, hay, or other coarse material. Remove the next spring after all danger of frost has passed.

SWEET POTATOES

Related to the morning glory, the sweet potato is a tender tropical vine that performs best in regions with long, hot summers. It needs full sun and about 120 days of warm temperatures.

Sweet potatoes are grown from slips, or sprouted cuttings; you can buy them at garden centers or from catalogs—or grow your own. About four to six weeks before planting time, place a sweet potato on a bed of sand and cover it with moist sand. Keep at 75°F until sprouts are about 6 inches tall and have roots and a few leaves. This "seed potato" will produce ten to twenty plants.

Some gardeners remove the new shoots and their roots by pulling or twisting them off. Others prefer cutting, which inhibits transfer of any diseases or pests.

Wait three to five days before planting slips; little root hairs will develop and help ensure survival. Also wait until the soil temperature reaches at least 65°F.

Make a mound by pushing soil to about a foot high and a foot wide; sweet potatoes will appreciate the good drainage. Plant the slips 4 inches deep at 12-inch intervals. Spacing at 15-inch intervals encourages early production.

The slips develop best in sandy loam, where they can expand with less effort than in clay. To promote root production instead of vine growth, loosen the soil well and dig in a low-nitrogen fertilizer, like 8–24–24, before planting.

Keep young plants moist, even though sweet potatoes need less water once they're established. Watering is especially important in fast-draining sandy soils, as is a midseason drink of liquid fertilizer; a good choice is liquid seaweed extract.

Weed carefully until plants become established; the shallow roots won't tolerate disturbance. Once the vines cover the soil, they will shade out weed seedlings, making heavy maintenance unnecessary.

Depending on the variety, tubers can be harvested three to four months after planting. In cold regions, the tubers are ready when frost blackens the vines.

Sweet potatoes are subject to bruising, which shortens their shelf life. Dig them up carefully with a spading fork. To help "set" the skin and make the tubers less susceptible, remove the vines a week before harvesting.

Brush but don't wash the soil off the potatoes before storing them. Clean with water just before you're ready to cook them; otherwise they will spoil. To prolong storage life, cure sweet potato tubers by exposing them to high temperatures (85° to 95°F) and high humidity for a week immediately after harvest. You can use either a cold frame or a heated room for this treatment. If you let the tubers sit for two months before cooking, more of the starch will convert to sugar. Your sweet potatoes will be all the more tasty.

Tubers will keep four to five months if stored in a cool place (55° to 65°F). Don't let the tubers touch, or they will rot. Never store in the refrigerator.

Outdoor storage is possible in warm climates. Place the tubers between layers of straw and cover with corn shucks.

The sweet potato weevil chews the leaves and bores into the tubers. To discourage infestation, keep the soil clear of debris. Spray with pyrethrum or methoxychor when pests are active and destroy any infected plants.

SWISS CHARD

Not only edible, red chard is also ornamental, sporting crimson stalks and crinkly green leaves laced with crimson veins. Plant among flowers, herbs, and other showy vegetables like flowering kale. Red chard sparkles when cloaked in autumn frost.

The more fertilizer and compost you give chard, the more it will grow. Dig in plenty of well-aged manure before planting. Once plants are 6 inches tall, feed with 5–10–5 fertilizer every month or so, using 3 ounces per 10-foot row.

The best tool for harvesting chard is your hands; simply break off the stem at its base. Don't use a knife, which might injure the inner stems and prevent further growth.

Prolong the harvest by picking the outer leaves, a few at a time, after the plants grow to 10 inches. A biennial that won't bolt in heat, Swiss chard will continue developing new leaves from the central stem all summer into autumn.

In mild-winter regions, leave chard in the ground and it will send up tender young leaves the next spring. Protect the crowns with a deep layer of straw or other mulch if temperatures dip below 20°F; even if tops die back, the plant should bounce back.

Eliminate weeding by mulching with black plastic; space plants a foot apart. Alternatively, you can cover the soil well with compost.

TARRAGON

Buy plants, not seeds. Tarragon seed in packets is that of Russian tarragon—a less-aromatic variety than French tarragon, whose seeds are sterile. For the true anise-scented herb with a "bite," buy plants of *Artemisia dracunculus* var. *sativa*. Not all garden centers distinguish between the two, so take care when buying. French tarragon has a strong, sweet smell; test by crushing a leaf between your fingers.

Because tarragon needs winter dormancy, it is treated as an annual in warm and hot climates; grow it elsewhere as a perennial. Its basic needs, however, remain the same: extremely well-drained, loose soil and plenty of light.

Tarragon likes to be snipped, so don't be afraid to cut back the tips; it keeps the plants full and bushy.

The herb's name is related to the Latin word for "dragon"—a reference to its serpentlike root system. Divide plants in spring every two years to untangle the roots and keep them vigorous.

THYME

Common thyme is the classic garden herb, but you can also grow varieties that smell of lemon, caraway, or nutmeg. Silver thyme has leaves banded in white, and woolly thyme has fuzzy foliage. Mother-of-thyme is a common name for several species that self-sow readily after blooming: *Thymus praecox* ssp. *articus, T. pulegiodes,* and *T. serpyllum.*

Warmth-loving thyme thrives in well-drained soil and full sun. Plant it around a stone or brick path so that it can take advantage of the reflected heat and light. You can also tuck it into a stone wall, which provides extra warmth and quick drainage.

Keep it neat. For bushy plants, prune back the stems in spring if you live in a cool climate; in warm areas, prune in fall. Replace plants when they start to die back in the center—usually after three to five years.

Thyme flowers, which bloom in white, lavender, pink, and magenta, lure bees. Place thyme wherever you need plants pollinated or want to watch bees at work.

Some thyme varieties, including caraway and coconut, are ground-hugging evergreens and like to sprawl. Use as a soft edging for borders or a fragrant filler between stepping-stones.

Using thyme for cooking means pruning off most of the blooms. If you want to admire the bountiful little blossoms, plant a thyme border or combine them with your ornamentals.

TOMATOES

Purchasing

Tomatoes are classified as either determinate or indeterminate. The first is a bush type and needs no staking; the fruits form at the stem tips and all mature around the same time. The second is the vining type, which requires pruning and staking; fruits grow along the stem and keep developing until halted by frost.

What do the letters mean? Tomatoes have been developed to resist specific problems, and the letters after the variety names indicate which pests and diseases the plant can withstand. "F" is for fusarium wilt, "n" is for nematodes, "v" is for verticillium wilt, and "t" is for tobacco mosaic virus.

Plan on two plants per person for general consumption. If you intend to can and freeze the tomatoes, add a few more.

Planting

Sow tomato seed about eight weeks before the first frost-free date. Use a seed-starting mix and place four or five seeds in each pot. Tomato seeds need temperatures around 75°F to germinate.

Once the second set of true leaves form, move the plants to a cooler environment—55° to 65°F at night. Keep them moist and fertilize with manure tea or fish emulsion weekly. This treatment lets plants develop slowly and prevents them from becoming lanky.

Tomatoes are ready to set out when they have five to seven leaves. Plants that have already produced flowers or fruit may have a more difficult period of adjustment.

If you live in a hot region, stagger the planting dates so that you won't lose the entire crop if a heat wave strikes. To help shade them, interplant tomatoes among taller crops, such as corn.

In cold climates, place your tomatoes by a wall or the side of the house that faces south or west; it will absorb the sun's heat during the day and radiate it at night.

Tomatoes prefer well-drained soil with plenty of organic matter and a near-neutral pH. Dig a hole a foot wide and put in a layer of compost or well-rotted manure mixed with a handful of bonemeal and 1 teaspoon epsom salt. Fresh banana peels will act as a kind of slow-release fertilizer in the planting hole, providing potassium and trace elements. Some gardeners even put a dead fish in the bottom of the hole. In hot climates, do as old-timers did and place a 5-inch layer of corncobs at the bottom; it is said to conserve moisture.

For best results, space tomatoes 2 feet apart, with 3 to 4 feet between rows. Even though plants can be grown closer together, in typical garden soil their yields won't be as high; they will also be harder to prune and fertilize.

Bury them deep. The soil should reach to the first set of true leaves; additional roots will form along the buried part of the stem.

Trench-plant leggy seedlings or any that have been grown in tall containers. Lay the root-ball on its side in a rectangular hole dug to a depth of at least 6 inches. Hold the stem erect while covering the root-ball and the lower part of the stem with soil.

Stake indeterminate tomatoes by installing a 6-foot stake before planting; place it 4 inches from the hole and drive it a foot deep. Alternatively, use steel-mesh cages, stretch a chicken-wire trellis along the row, or let vines climb on strings suspended from an overhead wire. Loosely hold plant stems to the supports with figure-eight loops of soft twine every foot or so. You can also use soft cloth or pantyhose—they're gentler on the stems and will provide more support for heavy vines.

Tomatoes will feed as needed if planted around a nutrient supply. Dig a hole 10 inches deep and 3 feet wide. Encircle the hole with a 2-foot-tall mesh cylinder and fill with well-rotted manure or compost. Then plant six tomatoes around it—either in cages a foot away or just next to the cylinder, tying them on for support. Water cylinder contents regularly.

Maintenance

Use fertilizer low in nitrogen, such as 4–8–4; too much nitrogen promotes foliage growth and makes fruits watery and bland. Once the fruit is set, side-dress lightly every four to six weeks.

Mulch plants 2 to 3 inches deep with hay, straw, buckwheat hulls, or shredded leaves to conserve moisture and suffocate weeds. Apply after the soil is already warm.

When the fruits begin showing color, add a spoonful of sugar to their water—the tomatoes will be sweeter and juicier. But go easy: Minimizing water while fruits ripen enhances their flavor.

Once every seven to fourteen days, crush some eggshells in a blender and add them to the water for your tomatoes; about six shells per quart is enough. The extra calcium aids growth at the leaf tips and blossom ends and prevents blossom-end rot.

Prune your plants by pinching out the suckers between the main stems and the branches. The suckers can be rooted in pots and transplanted to the garden to provide a second crop of tomatoes.

Compensate for blossom drop, which often occurs in cool, wet weather or on hot, windy days, by helping the remaining blossoms set fruit. On a day that's warm, calm, and dry, aid pollination by gently shaking the plant or tapping its stake.

You can protect tomatoes from aphids by surrounding plants with aluminum foil, shiny side up. As a bonus, the radiant heat will speed ripening of the fruits by about two weeks.

Cold nights? Keep plants cozy by flanking each one with two flat stones or tiles. They hold the sun's heat during the day and radiate it at night. You can also surround each plant with a manufactured self-standing plastic sleeve filled with water.

More heaters: Cover your tomatoes with plastic film laid over wire wickets; make sure the plastic is tall enough so that plants won't touch it. Close off the ends and secure to the ground with wire stakes.

About three weeks before the first frost, remove all flowers and any fruits that have not yet reached a quarter of their mature size; they won't mature before the season is over and will divert nutrients from fruits that are more developed.

Harvesting

For the best taste, pick tomatoes when they are nearly or fully ripe; they should have even color and be firm but not hard. And don't leave overripe fruits on the vine—they decrease overall productivity and may spread disease.

Always keep tomatoes at room temperature, shoulders up. Putting them in the refrigerator stops the ripening process cold.

After the first light frost, pick all the fruits. Let immature fruits that have begun to "pale out" ripen in indirect light at a temperature of 70° to 80°F. Be aware that small, green tomatoes will not ripen satisfactorily; use them instead for preserves, pickles, or relishes.

TULIPS

Purchasing

"Firm and fat" is how a healthy, quality tulip bulb should appear. Don't worry if the papery outer layer is tattered, but avoid bulbs with soft spots, bruises, or nicks.

Hybrid or species? The stately tulips that herald spring are hybrids—the result of 300 years of breeding. They offer the widest range of colors and flower forms but can suffer in hot summers and fail to bloom reliably after the first year. Species (or botanical) tulips are the wild European and Asian natives. They are smaller and hardier than the hybrids and will naturalize in the right spot for years of bloom.

Come fall, garden centers are stocked full of tulip bulbs—but often with only the most popular varieties. For species tulips and lesser-known hybrids, seek out catalogs from specialty bulb growers, who are more likely to carry rarities.

Species tulips usually have open, starlike blooms with a "wild" look that recalls their native mountain habitats. Use them in informal sites like rock gardens and give them room to spread. Try *Tulipa batalinii*, *T. clusiana*, *T. eichleri*, *T. humilis*, *T. praestans*, and *T. turkestanica*.

In addition to the new varieties introduced each year, you can buy a number of tulips that have been grown for centuries. Look for *T. tarda* (c. 1590), *T. clusiana* (1606), 'Zomerschoon' (1620), and 'Keizerskroon' (1750).

The Rembrandt tulip, named for the Dutch painter, has blooms that are streaked and flushed with a second color. While this feature was originally caused by an aphid-borne virus, it has been duplicated genetically and safely in modern Rembrandt tulips.

Need an eye-catching tulip for a special location? Look for *T. acuminata*, the fireflame tulip. The red-streaked yellow petals roll up vertically into thin, irregular shapes that resemble tongues of fire.

Most tulips need a period of cold dormancy for best bloom. But some will perform well in warm climates without needing to be chilled. Try *T. sylvetris*, *T. bakeri* 'Lilac Wonder', 'Blue Parrot', 'White Triumphator', or 'Sweet Harmony'.

Planting

While tulips can usually adjust to many soil types, they grow best in rich, quick-draining loam. To condition the soil, turn in compost or very well-rotted manure to a depth of 8 to 12 inches. Add bonemeal to the planting hole or bed.

The right spacing. Plant hybrid tulips with 6 inches of soil above the bulb tips. In light, sandy soil, set them 8 inches deep to ensure strong roots and good support for the stems; in heavy soil, plant only 4 to 5 inches deep. For species tulips, plant the bulbs at a depth 2 ½ times their diameter but no less than 4 inches deep. Space all tulips 6 to 8 inches apart.

Rigid or random? For lining a path, tulips look best in a single row—like a rank of soldiers. For a naturalistic look, let the bulbs fall where they may. But don't just toss them over your shoulder: put them in a bucket and spill them over the ground.

Plant bulbs in the wire-mesh cages sold at garden centers to keep gophers, moles, and voles at bay.

Plant tulips in a sunny location; light afternoon shade will help the blooms last longer. And make sure the plants are sheltered from wind; a strong breeze can snap the top-heavy stems.

Planting time: In cold climates, plant the bulbs between late September and the first frost, while the soil is still workable and roots can develop. In warm areas, wait until early December, when the ground is cooler.

Underplant tulips with low-growing flowers or ground covers that blossom simultaneously, such as forget-me-not, wallflowers, chamomile, or sweet alyssum. The long-stemmed tulips will emerge from a frothy bed of blooms.

Maintenance

Don't let the soil around tulips dry out. As a rule, water to a depth of an inch each week.

Once tulips emerge in spring, sprinkle a little 5–10–5 fertilizer on the soil around them and dig in lightly.

The first cut: On hybrid tulips, snip off spent flowers just below the bloom; leave the foliage in place to manufacture food for the bulb so it can rebloom the next year. On species tulips, don't cut the heads off; let them go to seed and spread.

Once a tulip's foliage has yellowed—usually in midsummer—cut it off and add it to the compost pile. In the meantime, hide the withering leaves by planting taller-growing annuals in front.

A second-year slump is common for some tulips; not every variety is a reliable repeat bloomer, even in ideal conditions. Lift the bulbs at season's end and discard. Or replant in an inconspicuous spot, where their less-than-perfect blooms won't matter.

For long-lasting bouquets, cut tulips in the morning. Select fairly tight buds with good color on the upper two-thirds; buds that are cut too green won't open. Before putting them in a vase, recut the stems at an angle while you hold them underwater.

Beware when handling cut tulips; the sap can cause a rash on sensitive skin.

TURNIPS

Turnips, rutabagas, and kohlrabi are all members of the cabbage family. The first two are true root vegetables; kohlrabi bulbs, which grow on top of the soil, are swellings in the stems.

To avoid tough turnips, plant them in spring three weeks before the last frost or in fall, two months before the first frost. These cool-weather vegetables can tolerate cold if well mulched, but they turn woody and bitter in temperatures over 75°F.

Plant turnips in rich, loose soil amended with any organic matter except manure, which turnips don't like. If needed, adjust the soil pH to a range of 5.5 to 6.8.

A bonus crop: Sow seed an inch apart in rows 1 to 1 ½ feet apart. When you thin plants to 4 inches apart, save the thinnings: You can use the tender little bulbs and leaf tops either raw or cooked.

Crave greens? Grow a turnip variety bred for its tasty leaves. To keep them coming, snip with shears to an inch above the ground when the tops reach 6 inches tall.

Provide shade for young plants by sowing seeds close to corn plants or trellis-grown pole beans, cucumbers, or squash.

Harvest turnips in spring when they reach golf-ball size. In warm climates, pull up the fall crop as you need it. In cold areas, harvest the plants and remove the tops, leaving a bit of stem. Don't wash off the soil, and store the bulbs in a cool, dark place.

UNDERGROWTH

When clearing overgrown ground to plant a new garden bed or lawn, extraordinary measures may be required to rid the area of stubborn weeds, brush, brambles, and vines.

You can rent heavy-duty tools designed specifically for cutting through undergrowth. A brush trimmer is similar to a string trimmer but has a toothed metal blade instead of a filament line; use it for woody growth 1 to 2 inches thick. For dense grass with brambles, you'll need a "brush hog," which resembles a lawn mower with a large front cutting deck.

An easy way to clear undergrowth from a small area is by smothering it. Cut down all the vegetation in spring. Cover the ground with black plastic and anchor the edges with boards or stones. At summer's end, remove the plastic and spade up any remaining plants.

Repeated cuttings will eventually weaken plants by denying them the chance to manufacture food. The best time to cut back brambles is late June; you may have to cut them over several years.

Salt will destroy many plants, but use it only at a distance from desirable specimens. Dig the soil away from the base of brambles and other growth, then cut the stems as close to the ground as possible. Pour a good dose of salt directly into the wounds but try not to spill any on the soil.

The last resort: Use herbicides to clear undergrowth that won't respond to cutting, pulling, or smothering—or those that shouldn't be touched, like poison ivy. First try organic herbicides made from fatty acids, not chemicals; they work on many weeds on contact and are the least toxic.

Synthetic herbicides: Use a selective herbicide, which is less likely to cause harm if it drifts onto desirable plants or is carried by runoff. A systemic product will circulate through the plant and won't affect the surrounding soil—but check the label for warnings: With some products, you may not be able to replant the soil for a while.

To destroy the occasional persistent weed that reappears after you've removed the undergrowth—a tuft of thistle, for example—cut it back to the ground in early spring. When it regrows, remove the bottom from a screw-top plastic seltzer bottle and place it over the plant. Spray herbicide through the bottle's opening and screw on the top. Wait a couple of weeks and repeat the treatment if needed.

VEGETABLE GARDENS

Planning

The sunniest spot in your yard is the best place to stake out your plot. Most vegetables need a minimum of six hours of sun daily.

Because vegetables like plenty of moisture, site your plot near a water source. But take note: Vegetables hate standing water. Keep them away from any low spots and rain runoff, where water can collect.

When preparing a new bed, skim off the top 2 inches of soil or sod and add it to the compost. Removing this topmost layer will eliminate weeds for years.

For maximum results, give vegetables the best possible home while they live their short, intense lives. Each year, till or spade 2 or 3 inches of compost or rotted manure about 8 inches deep into the soil until it is loose and friable. Work in a complete fertilizer and, if necessary, amend the soil pH to around 6.0 to 7.0.

Rows or beds? Decide what kind of plot you want. Rows are easy to tend and allow air to circulate but are less efficient than beds in their use of space. Beds, on the other hand, permit intensive planting and therefore higher yields. A disadvantage is that beds take more time to prepare, are more awkward to tend, and have poorer air circulation.

To make tending beds easier, keep them no wider than the spread of your arms—about 4 feet. Design a main path wide enough for a wheelbarrow, allowing about 3 feet, and add footpaths about a foot wide between beds. To suppress weeds and provide a clean place to walk, keep paths covered with straw, chopped leaves, boards, or bricks.

If space is limited for a separate plot, combine vegetables with your flowers. Some veggies, like ruby chard, purple broccoli, and scarlet runner beans, are handsome enough to hold their own.

Leave room for blooms. Flowers in the vegetable garden not only make it a more pleasant place to work but also have their uses. Many types attract beneficial insects like bees, ladybugs, and lacewings, while others may repel pests. Try butterfly weed, French marigolds, or fennel. For a bonus, plant edible flowers like nasturtiums and violets.

Small-garden strategies: Plant vertical crops, like pole beans and squash, which take up little ground space. Or plant dwarf varieties, such as 'Tom Thumb Midget' lettuce and 'Tiny Dill' cucumbers. Or create a patio garden, using the dwarf varieties specially bred for containers: tomatoes, cabbages, cucumbers, melons, and more.

Buying

Deciding how many plants to grow depends on how you use your garden. If you're keen on canning and freezing, add more plants than you would need for eating fresh. But be careful not to overplant any prolific producers, like summer squash and tomatoes.

Expand your horizons. Look for a few unusual vegetables, including imported and heirloom varieties, to add to your mainstays. Be adventurous and try out a new cultivar each year—particularly with tomatoes, which come in countless varieties.

Consider your conditions. In areas with short growing seasons, buy fast-maturing or cold-tolerant vegetables. In warm and hot climates, buy heat-tolerant varieties so that you can enjoy cool-weather favorites like lettuce. Also buy plants that are resistant to diseases common in your region.

Planting

For maximum sun, try laying out rows east to west, following the sun's transit. Plants in north-to-south rows may get too much shade as the sun passes over.

For high yields, use space wisely. After harvesting a cool-weather crop (peas or spinach, for example), replant the space with a warm-weather vegetable (green beans or summer squash). Interplant quick growers (radishes) with slower ones (tomatoes); the short-term crop will be up and out before the slow grower can crowd or shade it.

With poor keepers, such as lettuce, don't plant all at once. Instead, plant short rows at one-week intervals. Doing so means you'll have fresh pickings throughout the season.

Reserve the north end of your garden for perennial vegetables, such as asparagus, and tall, shade-casting plants, like corn. The rest of the space will be freed up for its yearly soil preparation and stay sunny through the growing season.

Crop rotation is essential for preventing a buildup of harmful soilborne microbes that prefer certain plants. For this reason, don't plant a vegetable or a member of its family in the same place year after year. Instead, divide the garden into sections and move the plants from one area to another. As a general rule, a plant should be replanted in its original spot only every three or four years.

Another advantage: Rotate crops to help balance soil nutrients between light and heavy feeders. An example: The first year, plant peas, which fix nitrogen in the soil. The next year, follow with nitrogen lovers such as cabbage and broccoli.

Maintenance

Vegetables can't tolerate competition from weeds. Monitor the garden weekly to pull up any invaders and mulch the soil well to suppress them.

Vegetables need an inch of water per week, whether from rainfall or watering. Moisture needs are most critical for leafy crops as they approach maturity, for fruiting vegetables as they set blooms (but not as the fruit ripens), and for root crops as the roots start to expand. Water young vegetables lightly but frequently, never letting their soil dry out completely.

Slow-maturing vegetables often benefit from a supplemental feeding halfway through the growing season. Side-dress lightly with a complete fertilizer, water with manure tea, or spray with a foliar food such as kelp extract.

WATER BARRELS

Collect rain and melted snow for use in the garden—it will come in handy during dry spells. Use a wine barrel, trash can, or any watertight container. You can also look in catalogs for special rain barrels with a lid molded to accept a downspout and a spigot for drawing off water.

For crystal-clear water, use a barrel made of an opaque material; otherwise light will penetrate and encourage algae growth. Also cover the container with a lid or board to keep out insects, debris, and pollutants.

A water diverter fitted between two sections of downspout channels water to the barrel as needed. When the barrel is full, flip up the diverter to make gutters work as usual.

Raise your barrel up on bricks or blocks so that you have enough room to draw water from the spigot into a pail. Cover the surrounding ground with gravel or a single layer of bricks—if water splashes out, it won't disturb the soil.

If you want to hide the barrel, set it in the ground under a downspout. Position it so that the rim is about an inch above soil level and you can cover the top to keep out debris. When you need water, scoop it out in a bucket or siphon it out with a hose.

WATER PLANTS

Water plants bring life, color, and beauty to a pond. If your local nursery doesn't carry a good selection, make the extra effort to seek out aquatics. Check in gardening magazines for specialty growers and catalogs. Ask a botanical garden or horticultural society for sources.

Each plant needs a minimum amount of space to thrive. Plan on three to six submerged plants per square foot of surface area. Cover half to two-thirds of the pond with surface plants.

No water garden is complete without water lilies. Tropical varieties bear the showiest blooms but tolerate cold only to 40°F. Hardy types have a more subtle appearance but can overwinter outdoors as long as their roots are below the ice level.

The exotic water platters (*Victoria* spp.)—puckered green saucers with purplish undersides and pink blooms—can reach 6 feet across. Grow only in large ponds and in water 75°F or warmer.

Wait a week after you fill your pond before adding plants. This will allow the water to warm and any chlorine to dissipate.

Newly purchased plants may harbor pest eggs or larvae. Rinse the plants in a stream of water, then immerse the roots in a container of water for two weeks. Add to the garden once you're sure the plants are uncontaminated.

To get a submerged plant into deep water, wrap the roots in a strip of sod tied with twine; weight with a pebble. Toss the plant in the water—it will sink and settle on the bottom.

Plant a surface plant in a plastic or wire basket with a stable base; line with a permeable fabric to hold in soil. Fill to an inch below the rim with garden soil mixed with well-rotted manure. Set in the plant so that its crown is just at soil level; top with an inch of gravel. Place the basket at the proper depth for the leaves to float.

To add a plant basket in the middle of a deep pond, wind two long ropes around the rim. Working with a partner, pull the ropes taut to suspend the basket over the water. Lower it into place, then slack off on the cord, letting the plant settle in its new position.

Anchor emergent plants in the soil around ponds or in shallow water. If the muck doesn't hold them down, pin the root-balls carefully with *U*-shaped wires. Alternatively, set stones around the stems until the roots take hold.

Discourage algae growth by removing all yellowed plant foliage and spent flowers. Cut back on fish food and be sure that garden fertilizer doesn't run off into the pond. Add submerged plants to filter the water. Copper sulfate will control severe algae, but it can also harm plants and fish.

Winter care: Hardy plants can withstand the cold as long as their roots don't freeze. If there's a chance the water will freeze down to the pond bottom, lift the plants—especially any tropical specimens. Then store the plants in a cool, frost-free place and keep their soil moist.

Water plants are remarkably untroubled by pests. Squirt off any aphids with a strong stream of water; fish will eat them. If you spot any trails left by leaf miners, cut off the affected foliage. And watch for delta moth larvae, which float on bits of leaves on the surface; simply scoop them out with a net.

Leaf spots are usually caused by fungal diseases. Spray the foliage of affected plants with Bordeaux mixture and remove and destroy infected leaves and stems.

WATERING

Rule number 1: Water deeply but infrequently. This delivers moisture down to the plant root zone—usually between 6 and 18 inches deep—and encourages deeper roots, which in turn need less water. One inch of water penetrates about 12 inches in sandy soil but only 4 inches in clay after twenty-four hours.

An exception to the rule: The roots of young plants are shallow. Water them lightly and more often than mature plants.

Rule number 2: Water in the morning. Less moisture will evaporate at the cooler temperatures. Plants will also be able to dry before nightfall—discouraging foliage diseases.

Keep leaves dry. Water only the soil around plants that are prone to fungal infections; these include roses, lilac, phlox, and squash. Getting the foliage wet with overhead watering can cause mildew, as well as fungus and other diseases.

Plants often wilt in intense sun but may not need watering. To avoid overwatering, wait until the next morning. If the plants are still droopy, water then.

In arid areas, don't waste a drop of precious water. Locate your foundation plants in the center of broad, shallow depressions, then direct water from the gutter downspouts into the trenches.

Make a custom waterer for a specimen plant. Perforate a 1-gallon plastic jug and bury it near the plant with its spout right at soil level. Fill the jug with water; it will seep out slowly and keep the roots moist.

Equipment

When buying a garden hose, look for three- or four-ply vinyl, nylon, or rubber that is reinforced with mesh and rated for high water pressure (up to 500 pounds per square inch). Also look for heavy-duty, cast-brass couplings.

Always coil up a hose after use—either over a hose hanger, around a hose reel, or in a cut-down plastic garbage can. It will keep the hose from becoming riddled with unwieldy kinks.

Protect your plants. Dragging a hose through the garden can crush your plants. Run the hose around guides: Use either wood or metal stakes or manufactured guides with a lip that prevents the hose from slipping up over the top.

If you have only one outside tap and need to hook up several hoses, buy a distributor device. It threads onto the tap and has four connectors for adding hoses.

Can't reach to water your hanging baskets? Buy a spray wand. The long, light pipe with a rosette head attaches to a hose and extends your reach by 3 feet.

A soaker hose is made from canvas or perforated plastic and seeps or sprinkles water along its entire length, wetting the soil 2 feet on either side. It is especially useful for vegetable garden rows. If you use it for trees and shrubs, circle it around the plant along the drip line. The hose can also be buried up to a foot deep; you can leave it in the soil indefinitely.

Low-volume irrigation systems slowly apply water directly to the ground, with no runoff and less evaporation. Water penetration can be controlled by varying the delivery of gallons per hour (gph).

Drip irrigation, using a network of plastic tubes with emitters that drip or spray water along their length, is the most efficient low-volume system. Start with a small kit, sold at garden centers and through catalogs.

WEEDS

A weed is any plant—even an ornamental—that grows where it's unwanted. Common weeds are fast-growing, resilient nuisances that not only make the garden look unsightly but also steal nutrients from your cultivated plants and serve as hosts for pests and diseases. Weeds can be annual, biennial, or perennial. Annuals and biennials reproduce only by setting seed—but a single plant can yield more than 10,000 seeds. Perennials also spread by roots and stems.

Weed seeds need light to germinate. To shade the soil around your plants, keep it covered with organic mulch, black plastic or paper mulch, layers of wet newspaper, or a geotextile weed mat.

Build a shield. Use edging materials like bricks or underground barriers of metal or plastic around garden beds. This will keep lawn grass and perennial weeds from creeping into flower beds and vegetable plots.

Solarizing the soil means letting the sun do the weeding work for you. Till up the soil and water it. Lay a sheet of clear plastic over the area, anchor the edges with stones, and wait four to six weeks: The sun's heat will "cook" weed seeds. If any weeds are found after you lift the cover, rake them up lightly without disturbing the soil.

Till twice. Till the soil the first time to bring buried weed seeds up to the surface, where they can germinate. Wait two weeks. Till again, this time with the tiller at a shallower setting. The second tilling will chop up the weeds without exposing more seeds.

Be careful with compost. Toss into the pile any weeds that have not yet bloomed; they have no seeds to spread. Add weeds that have set seed only if the pile heats up to 200°F—the temperature needed to kill seeds. Or start a separate compost pile for weeds; use this compost only in deep planting holes, where seeds can't germinate.

Keep soil covered. Don't let soil remain bare for any length of time—weeds will move right in. If you regrade or remove plantings, blanket the soil with a cover crop, ground cover, mulch, or grass.

Don't mow too short. Letting grass grow to the

recommended height shades out weed seeds. It also spurs root growth, which crowds out any emerging weeds.

Control

Don't automatically reach for the sprayer to treat lawn and garden weeds. A combination of elbow grease, ingenuity, and tools will usually do the job.

Buy a dandelion digger, which has a sharp, notched end that will pry up stubborn weeds with taproots. You can also buy weeding tools with hoelike blades and short handles; they're good for slicing weeds off below the surface.

Water before weeding. Weeds are easier to pull with their root systems intact if the soil is moist. Also, neighboring plants are less likely to be disturbed or damaged.

Use a hoe to shave the tops off weed seedlings by keeping the head parallel to the ground and pulling shallowly in the soil. Digging down can bring weed seeds to the surface and compact soil.

Take it all. Be sure to remove any part of the weed that can regenerate. Wild garlic grass will regrow from little bulblets, plantains have persistent taproots, and quack grass can resprout from its deep, spreading root system.

Sprinkle salt on weeds that sprout in paved areas or wild patches. But don't use it around your desirable plants.

Drench weeds growing up through the cracks in paving stones or bricks with boiling water. Some old-time gardeners insist that water from boiled potatoes is even more effective.

Herbicides

Start gently. Always try a product with low toxicity, such as an organic herbicidal soap, before using harsher poisons.

Keep cans separate. Reserve a single watering can, a sprayer, and measuring implements for using only with herbicides.

Be extremely careful when applying herbicides. Direct the product only at the weeds—not at desirable plants. Also make sure that there are no obstructions in a sprayer nozzle that could cause liquid herbicide to squirt out at an angle. Wait for a calm day to apply the chemicals so that wind doesn't carry the spray or granules to an unintended location.

Be weather-wise. Herbicides work best when temperatures are mild (70° to 80°F) and the soil is moist. Don't apply sprays before a rain, which will wash them away.

Use a preemergent herbicide on the lawn to keep weeds from sprouting and work it into cultivated soil before installing plants. It's especially useful in new patches of ground cover.

Toxic-free zone: Because a tree's roots are concentrated under the canopy, don't use herbicides to kill any weeds there. Instead, remove the weeds manually and cover the soil with an organic mulch.

Don't risk runaways. Take care when applying herbicides on the top of a slope if desirable plants are located below. Water runoff could carry the poisons where you don't want them to go.

You've poisoned a plant by accident? If so, water it immediately and thoroughly to flush out the chemicals. Continue watering daily for a week to limit the damage.

WISTERIA

Wisteria is a fast-growing climbing vine that produces heavily scented cascades of white or lavender blooms in late spring. But it is also a willful beauty that can quickly outgrow its bounds and latch onto gutters, shingles, and shutters. Be aware that wisteria can literally pull apart all but the strongest trellis. Don't plant wisteria near your house, trees, or utility lines, where it could become a nuisance. Instead, train it to twine along a strong fence or over a stone wall. Chinese and American wisterias twine up a support from left to right; Japanese and formosan wisterias twine from right to left.

Feed young wisteria extra fertilizer to help it become established. Mature plants bloom better without supplements.

Regular and careful pruning not only keeps wisteria contained but also promotes next year's blooms. Clip after flowering in summer by cutting off the long, stringy shoots to 6 inches, leaving six leaves (the buds form on short spurs); prune again in winter, shortening the shoots to 3 inches with three buds. Also snip off any side shoots emerging from the base of the trunk.

Train as a tree. You can train wisteria as a standard by staking it upright and pruning the top heavily for years. The stem will eventually grow to trunklike proportions.

Root-prune wisteria vines that fail to flower; forcing roots to branch out encourages flower bud formation. Use a spade to cut a circle about 4 feet in diameter (smaller for young vines) and 2 to 3 feet deep around the trunk, cutting off any roots you encounter there.

XERISCAPING

Xeros is the Greek word for dry: Thus "xeriscaping" is landscaping that requires very little, if any, supplementary water. Ideally, a xeriscape garden is built with plants that naturally thrive on the normal rainfall of the region.

Xeriscaping saves in two ways. After your plants have become "conditioned"—usually about two years—you won't have to spend time watering. A drip irrigation system will also save on water bills.

Planning

Xeriscaping doesn't limit your garden to cacti and rocks. On the contrary, a well-designed xeriscape can be eye-catching and lush all year. If you limit the size of the garden, you can set aside a small portion for vegetable and cutting gardens, which demand more water.

Avoid desert xeriscapes with large areas of gravel and only a few succulents for interest. Such a spare layout offers no respite from the sun; in fact, it raises the temperature by radiating heat back into the environment.

A trickling fountain is a refreshing addition to a xeriscape garden in the hot, dry areas of the Southwest. Even the sound of splashing water is restful. A recirculating pump keeps water use to a minimum.

Lawn is allowed. Lawns require more water than most ground covers, but you can save water by confining your turf to a single focal point off the patio or between flower beds. Choose dryland grass species that need less water—tall fescues, blue grama, and buffalo grass; adjust your mower so that you don't cut the blades too short. Elsewhere in the garden, replace your lawn with drought-tolerant ground covers, such as common yarrow, Portuguese broom, and sea thrift.

Annuals adaptable to xeriscaping in both warm and cold climates include marigolds, cockscomb, African daisy, dusty miller, gazania, moss rose, sunflowers, and zinnias.

Planting

Hill soil around the base of new trees and shrubs to create a water-catching basin. Water infrequently and deeply to encourage deep roots. After two years, you can knock down the basins and install a low-volume irrigation system.

Dryland plants do best in raised beds that shed excess water. Work with the plant's natural defense against drought by mixing an absorbent amendment like pumice into the bed. After a rain, plants will absorb water released by the pumice long after the soil has dried.

Peat moss worked into the soil will make bare-root dryland plants root faster.

Zone your xeriscape garden according to the water needs of the plants. Group those that need more moisture, for example, where they can benefit from the runoff water from downspouts, driveways, and patios. Put plants that don't need full sun under the dappled shade of tall trees; this will keep the soil temperature down and minimize the need for water.

Put plants in the ground just before the rainy season to take advantage of whatever natural precipitation you get. Space them far enough apart so that roots will have plenty of room to spread and won't have to compete for moisture.

Maintenance

Use mulch. By keeping soil temperatures cool, a 2- or 3-inch layer of organic mulch significantly reduces water loss.

Low-volume irrigation systems operate at low pressure and deliver a low but steady amount of water. They include soaker hoses, controlled drip emitters, miniature sprayers and sprinklers, and root irrigators that soak the soil beneath the surface.

Electronic timers are available that will water your garden whether you're at home or away. Invest in one and hook it up to your low-volume system.

YUCCA

Tough and resilient, the yucca can put up with drought, heat, cold, and poor soil, and still produce spectacular creamy white flowers once a year. Its many varieties are grown in gardens, on patios and terraces, and in sunrooms throughout every part of the country; some species are hardy to 0°F. Because yucca leaves die down and remain attached to the trunk, they won't fall off and dirty the water of swimming pools and ponds.

The Joshua tree is said to have been named by early missionaries who were reminded of the prophet Joshua by the tree's uplifted arms. Buy this yucca in a container; it can be hard to establish if bare-root.

Dry leaf tips? Don't worry. They are common to yuccas and do not indicate an illness or infestation.

A healthy yucca has no spots on the leaves at its center.

If you do see spots, they indicate bugs or fungus. Treat by spraying the plant with malathion or a fungicide.

When temperatures rise above 85°F, you can give yuccas a little water and watch them thrive. When the weather cools, however, water only every two weeks.

ZINNIAS

Sow zinnias, an easy annual, in peat pots about four weeks before the last frost is predicted; seeds will sprout in four or five days. Harden off the seedlings for a few days in a cold frame or other sheltered place before setting them out. Then plant, peat pots and all, directly in the ground; zinnias don't like to have their roots disturbed.

When seedlings have three pairs of leaves, thin them out. Remove the weakest seedlings, leaving 6 inches between smallest varieties, 10 inches between medium-sized ones, and 18 inches between the tallest types.

"Cut-and-come again" was an old name used for zinnias, which respond enthusiastically to cutting. Deadheading fading flowers and cutting fresh ones for display will keep the plants amazingly prolific. Choose buds that are just about to open and cut them early in the day. Before putting them in a vase, strip off the lower leaves, which can quickly deteriorate.

Don't wet the leaves. Zinnias like moist soil but are subject to mildew. To prevent the problem, keep the leaves dry.

Apply a 5–10–5 fertilizer, scratching it carefully into the soil around the plants. It will improve the quality of the blooms and increase their number.

Stalk borers may tunnel into zinnias. Cut open the affected stems and dig out the intruders. If treated right away, the plant will probably survive.

Reader's Digest Quintessential Guide

ZUCCHINI

Zucchini are famous for producing more squash than even a large family can use. If your climate is conducive to such a surplus, take extra produce to a soup kitchen or share it with your friends.

To get an early crop, sow zucchini indoors in late April in the North or three weeks earlier in the South. Transplant the seedlings to a sunny part of the garden a month later to be ready for a harvest by July 4.

Pick fruits when they measure from 4 to 6 inches long. Once they've grown past 8 inches, their skin hardens and their flesh is full of seeds.

Bush-type plants, such as 'Ambassador', 'Aristocrat', 'Butterstick', and 'Seneca Milano', take up less room than the older vining varieties and don't need staking. Other popular compact types are 'Long Green Striped' and 'Zucchini Select'.

Round zucchini: Scan your catalogs for 'Ronde de Nice', a round heirloom variety the size of a tennis ball. It makes a unique side dish when stuffed with bread crumbs.

Try courgettes. Zucchini are called courgettes in much of the world. In America, the term is usually applied to baby zucchini, whether young fruits or dwarf cultivars. Harvest courgettes at 2 to 3 inches with the flowers still attached; slit them lengthwise and sauté lightly. Look for 'Type 1406', a seedless Swiss variety.

Also Available from Reader's Digest

The most useful information in a most useful format, from the people who have been getting to the heart of the matter for almost 100 years.

Reader's Digest Quintessential Guides—
The Best Advice, Straight to the Point!

Expect the Unexpected—Know What to Do When You Need to Do It

- Prevent and handle accidents
- Cope with medical situations
- Quick repairs you can do yourself
- Stock the right supplies
- Keep your family safe

$14.99 • Concealed Spiral • 978-1-62145-250-8

An A to Z of Ingenious Tips for Stretching Your Dollars

- Cut household bills
- Spend less on groceries (and eat better!)
- Find unexpected sales and freebies
- Make the most of your health care
- And much more!

$14.99 • Concealed Spiral • 978-1-62145-248-5

The Truth Behind the Foods We Eat and What to Choose for Optimum Health

- The enemies of good nutrition and the food heroes revealed
- Discover the links between good food, good health, and long life
- Tips on shopping, storing, preparing, and serving

$14.99 • Concealed Spiral • 978-1-62145-293-5

Reader's
digest

For more information, visit us at RDTradePublishing.com.
E-book editions are also available.

Reader's Digest books can be purchased through retail and online bookstores.